THRICE
THE BRINDED CAT
HATH MEW'D

THRICE

THE BRINDED CAT

A Record of the Stratford

CLARKE, IRWIN & COMPANY LIMITED, TORONTO

ROBERTSON DAVIES

TYRONE GUTHRIE

HATH MEW'D

Shakespearean Festival in Canada 1955

BOYD NEEL

TANYA MOISEIWITSCH

CONTENTS

ACKNOWLEDGMENTS

THE QUOTATIONS from W. B. Yeats' translation of 'Oedipus Rex' are from *The Collected Plays of W. B. Yeats*, published by Macmillan & Company Limited, and have been used here with the permission of Mrs. Yeats, the publishers, and The Macmillan Company of Canada Limited.

ILLUSTRATIONS

Julius Caesar

The Merchant of Venice

King Oedipus

PREFACE

NAMING A BOOK is an even greater problem than naming a child, for in the case of the child you begin with a surname already found. The anxious parents want a name that is euphonious and of good omen for their darling; the authors, no less anxious, want a name of similar merits for their book. There are a few obviously inspired and inevitable book-titles, like *Anna Karenina* and *The A B C of Acid Base Chemistry*, but usually the title of a book is chosen after much inward prayer and debate, and the author may suffer misgivings about his choice long after the book has appeared. Some of our readers may find it odd that this book should be called *Thrice the Brinded Cat Hath Mew'd*; perhaps they would like to know how that title was chosen.

The task of naming the two earliest books about the Shakespeare Festival at Stratford, Ontario, fell to my lot, and I chose *Renown at Stratford* for the first, and *Twice Have the Trumpets Sounded* for the second. Both titles derived from plays which were performed in the festivals recorded, and both titles were open to objection as being somewhat pompous; this objection was forcibly expressed to me on more than one occasion by my co-author, Dr. Tyrone Guthrie, and though I admitted the fond impeachment I defended myself by saying that my invention would run to nothing better, and if he didn't like them why didn't he think up the titles himself, and so on, in the rancorous manner common to authors.

The choice of *Twice Have the Trumpets Sounded* was

greatly influenced by the facts that it celebrated a second festival which was a marked success, that trumpets (and something which is either a French horn or an euphonium) are sounded before each Festival performance, and that the quotation came rather neatly from *Measure for Measure*. But in 1955 the plays afforded no comparable quotation with any hint of the number three in it. There was, of course,

Thrice hath Calpurnia in her sleep cried out

but this was by no means ideal, and the fact that the succeeding line is

Help, ho! They murder Caesar!

might have been interpreted as an unfavourable comment on the Festival's production of *Julius Caesar*. I was stumped, and from the depths of my misery I suggested that

Thrice the brinded cat hath mew'd

from Act IV, Scene one of *Macbeth* would have to be the name of the new book. I meant this as a joke, and also as a broad hint that I expected somebody else to find a title.

The joke was much better received than I had expected. Dr. Guthrie liked it, and so did Miss Tanya Moiseiwitsch; Dr. Boyd Neel maintained a sphinx-like reserve, but he did not say me nay. So we all backed this title, certain in our hearts that the publisher would never permit it.

The publisher, however, had an incalculable sense of humour. When the authors met him for the last time on June 16, on the verandah of Dr. Guthrie's house in Stratford, he declared in favour of that title. It stirred the imagination, he said, and it was certainly not pompous. Why should we not have a little fun at our own expense?

The late W. H. Clarke was a wise and experienced publisher. These books about the Stratford Festival were very near to his heart, and he regarded them as a means of spreading knowledge of the Festival beyond the ranks of those who were able to attend it, and also as permanent records of a movement which will be of historic importance in the development of the theatre in Canada. To this end, he directed their format and their illustration with a lavishness and care far greater than would be justified in any primarily commercial venture. His death on July 31 was a deprivation to many artistic causes, and anything which is a reflection of his personality and influence in this direction should be preserved if possible. Therefore the authors are happy to perpetuate this pleasantry of his in the title of the present volume.

Mr. Clarke was careful that these books should not be repetitive, and this one is not precisely in the mould of either of the others. It includes some consideration of the musical side of the Festival, which was a new departure in 1955; the illustrations are reproduced from the working designs made by Miss Moiseiwitsch for the use of the costumers and artificers at Stratford; the designer and Dr. Guthrie have collaborated in the portion of the book which gives some insight into the actual processes of putting a classical play on the stage.

The essays on the productions themselves are somewhat more critical in tone than they have been in the other two books, for the Festival is now of sufficient artistic stature to allow of such an approach—which might have sounded like ungenerous niggling if it had been attempted earlier. I saw the three plays more than once, and have attempted, in Postscripts to the essays, to give

xi

some notion of what happened to the productions in the course of the Festival.

For anyone who does not know what a brinded cat is, it may be explained that it is a cat marked with streaks of a colour somewhat darker than its body-colour—a tabby-cat, in fact. The authors are not prepared to entertain suggestions that a fourth volume in this series —if such there should be—ought to be called

Thrice and once the hedge-pig whin'd

even though this is what follows in *Macbeth*. The brinded cat will pass, but a hedge-pig might, in a favourite phrase of Dr. Guthrie's, be going too far.

ROBERTSON DAVIES

October 1
1 9 5 5

JULIUS CAESAR

By ROBERTSON DAVIES

JULIUS CAESAR
by WILLIAM SHAKESPEARE

FLAVIUS	Bruce Swerdfager	CAESAR'S SERVANT	Jim Manser
A CARPENTER	David Gardner	ARTEMIDORUS	Bruno Gerussi
MARULLUS	Bruno Gerussi	PUBLIUS	Alex de Naszody
A COBBLER	Ted Follows	POPILIUS LENA	David Gardner
JULIUS CAESAR	Robert Christie	ANTONY'S OFFICER	Neil Vipond
CASCA	Douglas Campbell	OCTAVIUS' OFFICER	Robert Goodier
CALPURNIA	Eleanor Stuart	CINNA THE POET	William Hutt
MARK ANTONY	Donald Davis	OCTAVIUS CAESAR	Donald Harron
A SOOTHSAYER	Roland Hewgill	M. AEMIL. LEPIDUS	John Hayes
MARCUS BRUTUS	Lorne Greene	VOLUMNIUS	Peter Haworth
CASSIUS	Lloyd Bochner	PINDARUS	Bruno Gerussi
CICERO	Edward Holmes	CAMP POET	David Gardner
CINNA	Tony van Bridge	MESSALA	Tony van Bridge
LUCIUS	William Shatner	TITINIUS	Douglas Rain
DECIUS BRUTUS	Douglas Rain	VARRO	Edward Holmes
METELLUS CIMBER	Eric House	CLAUDIUS	Eric House
TREBONIUS	Grant Reddick	DARDANIUS	Bruce Swerdfager
PORTIA	Barbara Chilcott	CLITUS	Ted Follows
LIGARIUS	William Hutt	YOUNG CATO	Roland Bull

CITIZENS, SENATORS, ATTENDANTS, SOLDIERS: Guy Belanger, William Cole, Julian Flett, Robin Gammell, John Gardiner, Robert Gibson, Peter Henderson, John Horton, Richard Howard, Charles Jolliffe, Jim Manser, Harry McGirt, Louis Negin, Ken Pauli, Peter Perehinczuk, Thurston Smith, Orest Ulan, Russell Waller, Beverley Wilson, Alan Wilkinson, Allan Zielonka, Aimé Aunapuu, Nomi Cameron, Pauline Galbraith, Margaret Griffin, Barbara Franklin, Roberta Kinnon, Irene Moszewska, Gertrude Tyas, Joan Watts, Lynn Wilson.

The action of the play takes place in Rome near Sardis and the plains of Philippi.

DIRECTED BY MICHAEL LANGHAM
DESIGNED BY TANYA MOISEIWITSCH
MUSIC BY LOUIS APPLEBAUM
BATTLE SCENES ARRANGED BY DOUGLAS CAMPBELL

ALTHOUGH THIS PLAY is always spoken of as a tragedy, it is written in the form of a chronicle, and this confusion about its nature creates special difficulties for the director and the actors. It contains, in Caesar and Brutus, two characters who might well have been tragic heroes, and in the roles of Cassius and Antony it provides two more parts so full of opportunities that they can hardly be reckoned as of lesser importance. Four leading parts, none of which is clearly superior to the others, make for difficulties of balance in putting the play on the stage. And thus, although a satisfactory presentation of the play must always be a rich experience in the theatre, the audience is not left with the sense of having seen the completed tragedy of one great character developed to its fullest measure, as they would do in the case of a good performance of, for instance, *Coriolanus.*

It is doubtful if most playgoers nowadays care greatly about this confusion in the nature of the play, though it was a frequent complaint against it in the eighteenth century. We are more content than were some of our ancestors to take it as it is. The production at Stratford stressed the chronicle elements in *Julius Caesar,* and the stage there made it possible to move the action along at full Elizabethan speed. And thus the play, which many of us have seen as a not completely satisfactory tragedy on the proscenium stage, took on a different character and revealed a welcome strength and urgency as a history play.

We were always conscious, however, that we were watching a play in which there were characters closely akin to Shakespeare's great tragic heroes. Brutus falls only a little short of that magnitude. He has been much admired and discussed by scholars, and it may well be that he looks better in the study than he does on the stage. We must, in such a record of a stage performance as this, judge by the standards of the theatre, and it is a fact that, whatever glories we can discover in Brutus when we think about him, he cannot dominate the play completely in the theatre, unless the play is distorted to allow him to do so. There is no instance in stage history of an actor making a great reputation in this role. And if we believe that Shakespeare knew his business as a playwright, we must assume that he did not mean Brutus to stand high above the other characters in *Julius Caesar*.

SHAKESPEARE AND HIS ROMANS

OF COURSE IT IS IDLE to speculate about the plays that Shakespeare did *not* write. Nevertheless, we may assume that he knew many things about the historical Brutus which he did not use in the play. He has not shown us Brutus the Usurer, which was an aspect of the hero bitterly familiar to many unhappy people of his time; that the man who accused Cassius of having 'an itching palm' was himself one of the notable Scrooges of history is an irony which Shakespeare would certainly have appreciated. A touch of weakness along these lines would have made Brutus more interesting than he appears in the play, where he exhibits an almost oppressive degree of unrelieved nobility. It seems probable, too, that Shakespeare was aware that Brutus was quite possibly the illegitimate son of Julius Caesar—a circumstance which would give special poignance to the dictator's dying cry of 'Et tu, Brute?' Shakespeare could have given us a great play about the jealousy between fathers and sons, about jealousy disguised as republican zeal, and about the patricidal element in revolution, if he had chosen to

4

do so. But the play he wrote was *Julius Caesar* as we have it, and a noble play it is. Therefore, if he chose to make Brutus slightly less than a full-fledged tragic hero, are we to assume that it was because he could not do so? The playwright who had just completed *Henry V* and three of his finest comedies, and who was approaching the creation of *Hamlet*, would not be likely to fail in his full intentions toward Brutus.

The chronicle nature of the play makes the assassination of Caesar a central, rather than a culminating, element in the plot, and it is part of the playwright's A B C that he cannot have a hero who vanishes from the action at the beginning of the third of his five acts. True, Caesar appears again as a ghost, and one of the many fine imaginative strokes in the Stratford production was to give him two later ghostly appearances when, at fateful moments, the murdered conqueror in his bloody mantle moved stealthily among the living. But a ghost is not a hero.

Shakespeare has not chosen to show us Caesar in a heroic aspect. He has taken pains to do otherwise. Great men of history, put on the stage, are taken by the audience at their full historical value unless something is done very plainly to diminish their greatness. A score of mediocre plays and movies about Napoleon, in which he never does or says anything Napoleonic, but is stopped short of obvious stupidity, prove the point; tell us that an actor with a forelock and a pillow in the front of his breeches is Napoleon, and our imagination, if not too rudely outraged, will sustain the illusion. Shakespeare could have let us think Caesar great. But he has shown us the great man complaining of infirmity, and boasting in a fashion that cools our sympathies. This Caesar is the focus of attention whenever he is on the stage, but he is shown to us as a superman who has begun to run to seed. Although the part is a fine one and admirably effective, nobody can argue that it is intended as the mainspring of the play.

Neither Caesar nor Brutus rises to full tragic height, and on the slightly lower level on which they stand, they are very close to Cassius and Antony. Cassius is no hero, but he is a man of interesting and sympathetic character; we cannot fully like him or admire him, but we can like and admire parts of him, and we can argue about him endlessly, as we cannot about Brutus. His combination of republican patriotism and jealousy, his fiery temperament, his weakness in the matter of money, and his hard-bitten acceptance of his fate unite to make a character extremely effective on the stage, and a challenge to the supremacy of the other three principal actors.

Antony, similarly, is not great but has qualities of attraction which the honourable Brutus lacks. We cannot fully like him, for the same reason that we cannot like Prince Hal; he is too sharp, too calculating in his dealings with others. We are moved by his emotion over Caesar's body and his pledge to revenge his friend; but we cannot like the way in which he turns that revenge to his own purposes. And although the scene in which he turns the Mob against the slayers of Caesar is one of the most superbly effective in all drama, we watch it under special circumstances, for we are not ourselves moved by it to hate the conspirators. It is always somewhat distasteful to see other people being moved by oratory which does not move us, and in this great scene we must recognize that Shakespeare is up to his old game of showing the Mob as fickle and stupid. The man who fools them so completely is not a man we can fully like or trust. But he is a man who holds our attention, and many a star actor of the past has considered Antony the best part in the play.

6

Julius Caesar, then, is a play which is written like a chronicle, but which contains one role of near-tragic stature, and another which—because Caesar was a world-conqueror and a creature of legend—is necessarily very strong competition to it; in addition there are two other parts which are of unusual interest and strongly threaten the two obvious leads. Such a play bristles with problems for the director.

A SENSE OF IMPERIAL ROME

AT STRATFORD MR. MICHAEL LANGHAM gave us a stirring realization of the play, filled with life and a sense of the action taking place in the heart of a great empire. The Crowd was as important an element in this production as the Chorus in a Greek play. Indeed, we may say that the Crowd added a fifth vital element to the four great roles which, in the printed text, dominate the play. Whether this was an entirely happy state of affairs is a matter for debate; there are those who argue that if Shakespeare provides lines for four Citizens to speak, he wants four Citizens on the stage and not, as in this production, forty. My own feeling is that the people who think along these lines should join forces with those who think that we should painstakingly reproduce the inadequate choirs and inept string-players who first performed the works of J. S. Bach. Good taste and artistic discretion must be the guides in such matters. If the Crowd in *Julius Caesar* threatened, at times, to swamp the production, it was a fault of generosity and exuberance.

The Crowd was the first thing to impress us in the production, for the play opened with citizens, soldiers and peasant women in a pattern of movement which admirably suggested the life of a great city, and gave us a sense of the courage of Flavius and Marullus in

7

attempting to quell their enthusiasm. Under these circumstances, it must be noted, the threadbare witticisms
of that Cobbler who is one of Shakespeare's most hapless
comics appeared to unusual advantage; this, we felt,
was the way the mind of the Crowd worked, and people
who could laugh at such jokes were ripe for the tricky
oratory of Antony or anybody else who could tickle
their ears.

We were struck at once by the colour and richness of
the costumes and appurtenances of the play, which gave
weight to the impression of Imperial Rome. The balance
between Roman costume as it was, and as Shakespeare
probably conceived it, was managed with skill. This
play abounds in references to doublets, hats and other
articles which do not fit easily into a strictly archaeological
production. But when the play is dressed in Elizabethan
costume, as sometimes happens, it looks silly to modern
eyes. The Stratford production was rich in colour, not
forceful but subtle in its tones, which gave it a substan-
tially Roman appearance. Perhaps because their statuary
has come down to us scoured white by wind and weather,
we are apt to think of the Romans as a bleached people;
a very little study of their painting tells us that they
made the fullest use of all the colours which may be seen
on the Mediterranean coast today. It is easier to believe
in the passions which rage in *Julius Caesar* when we see
it acted in full colour than when we see all the players
dressed in what (however we struggle to banish the dis-
respectful thought) look to us like blankets.

On the Stratford stage, where scenery is impossible,
great care is always given to the appurtenances of a
production, as was also the case in the Elizabethan theatre.
Imperial Rome delighted in banners and the insignia
of power, and it was a pleasure to see these handsomely
realized. A great golden spreadeagle mounted on a pole;

8

a ponderous standard with the *Senatus Populusque Romanus* symbol; golden wreaths and sheaves of wheat borne in procession; the splendid sceptre of Caesar himself, and the handsome chair in which he was carried; the banners topped with busts; the armour and weapons of the soldiers; these things, no less than the bearded priests of Jupiter, and the slaves and foreigners among the crowd, gave us the feel of Rome, and made us forget that we were watching a stage filled with actors, many of whom we were to see in more than one part.

There was a lush quality about the dressing and decoration of this production which was admirably evocative of Rome, but which also suggested one of the pitfalls of the Stratford stage. It was designed to free the director and the actors from the tyranny of scenery, and to give scope to the imagination of the audience, encouraged by the poetry of Shakespeare. When the poet wants us to believe that the action of a scene is in a specific place —a garden or a seashore—he describes it; when the location is of no importance he says nothing about it. The Stratford stage, which is modelled on an Elizabethan stage in many important respects, enjoys this freedom. In *Julius Caesar* there were times when we wondered if too much was not being done to suggest the location of a scene; this was particularly the case in the scene in Brutus' Tent, which would have been quite as effective without the drapery which was somewhat laboriously hung from the permanent balcony of the stage. The portable properties which suggested the pompous wealth of Rome were finely effective; but some of the more solid decoration, such as the tent, and the shattered statue of Pompey, were more trouble than they were worth. It is precisely to escape from such encumbrances that the Stratford stage was devised.

9

CAESAR

CAESAR'S GHOST

As we watched this play we were very rarely uncon-
scious of the hand of the director, and from time to time
we found ourselves too little conscious of individual
actors. There were good reasons why this should be so.
This was Michael Langham's first encounter with a stage
which presents special difficulties; everything that is
presented on it must be seen from three sides, and a
large part of the audience looks down on the stage, so
that the choreographic effects must be carefully considered, as well. The director must keep his actors in
movement much of the time, so that everybody can see
them, and it is easy to create a sense of restlessness which
has no real relation to the action. Mr. Langham's faults
were not those of a dull or confused director; he gave us
nothing that was trivial or fussy. His errors were all
attributable to a splendidly theatrical and inventive
mind which was determined not to be defeated by an
unfamiliar and difficult stage. By next year he will have
taken the measure of that stage to a hair's breadth, and
will know exactly how to use it, but in *Julius Caesar* he
somewhat overshot his mark.

The acting insufficiency must be attributed in a large
part to the fact that Mr. Langham had to deal with a
cast which had already been chosen. This could not
have been avoided, under the circumstances, but it was
unfortunate. A director casts a play in an individual
manner, and the way in which he disposes of his forces
rests on subjective judgements. Where two actors of
undoubted ability are available for a part, one director
will choose one, and another director will choose the
other, and neither may be able to explain satisfactorily
why he does so. It is enough that he feels that he can
work better with one man, and secure the effects that

he wants while helping the actor to give a good performance. We cannot envy Mr. Langham, given the job of putting a difficult play on a difficult stage, with a cast which he had not chosen for himself.

FINE ACTING IN MINOR ROLES

As THOUGH TO CONTRADICT this criticism, it is possible to recall at once a number of performances in supporting roles which were memorable for their excellence. Donald Harron, for instance, as Octavius Caesar, gave us a brilliant portrait of that chilly, calculating, thin-blooded youth. There are some very young men who are either so untroubled by human passion, or so lacking in emotional vitality, that they seem to have skipped youth and achieved old age before their time. Mr. Harron chose to make Octavius one of these, and his pale and thin-lipped face, his cold and precise utterance, and the reptilian glint in his eye marked him as a man of immoderate and ruthless ambition. Once again the strength of the Stratford company was shown; in how many companies could an actor of this quality be found to play Octavius? And how the play is illuminated when this secondary role is played with this degree of skill!

The same comment must apply to the acting of Douglas Rain as Decius Brutus and Titinius. He could bring to them a power of feeling and a distinction which greatly enriched the play. As parts, they are not of great consequence, and if they are indifferently played we hardly notice them. But when they were played as Rain played them, with a fine voice and the emotional intensity of an actor capable of playing much bigger roles, what strength they provide! So too with Tony van Bridge as Messala, and Bruno Gerussi as Pindarus; such actors as these are the foundation stones upon which a production of the

13

first order can be built. They have the experience and the power to realize them fully, and they have the artistic discretion not to overplay them. It would be unfair to comment on this matter without mentioning the performances of Eric House as Metellus Cimber, and William Shatner, who played Brutus' attendant, Lucius. All the minor roles in this production were played in a manner which was more than simply adequate; the high quality of the company let light into unexpected places, and revealed nuances in the play which are too often untouched.

WOMEN POORLY SERVED

THIS IS ONE of the Shakespearean plays which gives little opportunity for actresses. The Elizabethans, unlike ourselves, did not expect a display of female talent and probably beauty as well when they went to the theatre; their boy actors were undoubtedly competent, and perhaps better than that, but their emotional appeal, where it existed, was neither so strong nor so widespread as that of the actresses who invaded the English stage in 1660. To our Elizabethan ancestors a play with two minor women's roles in it was as acceptable as any other, and if Calpurnia and Portia were not quite up to the mark no great harm was done. But we look for their appearances as a relief from the endless procession of men. Mr. Langham took account of this modern predilection, and introduced two charming young women into the scene where Octavius and Antony are deciding which of their enemies shall die; these youthful ornaments were intended to bolster up Antony's reputation as 'a masquer and a reveller', as in the course of a short and busy scene he found time to toy very briefly with one of them, and they also gave a sense of the luxury of Rome, for they

CASSIUS

were splendidly undressed. There were women in the Crowd, as well, a circumstance which seemed less strange to us than it would have done to an audience in Shakespeare's day.

Calpurnia, the unfortunate wife of Caesar, has little opportunity to establish herself. She appears at the beginning of the play only in order to be publicly insulted by her husband. Later, she tries to dissuade him from going to the Senate-house, and is laughed at for her pains. Miss Eleanor Stuart played this ungrateful role as well as it could be played. Portia, the wife of Brutus, has a slightly better opportunity to impress herself on the audience; she has speeches of touching nobility, and to the present writer at least her declaration that she is—

A woman well reputed; Cato's daughter.

—always seems to open a door behind which stands all the republican pride and *gravitas* of Rome. Miss Barbara Chilcott played Portia with grace and dignity.

But both of these actresses seemed to suffer especially from the restless spirit of the production. They were in continual movement, and consequently there was uneasiness about their scenes, when we would have welcomed a quality of repose. The bustle of production on an Elizabethan stage is admirable in many ways, but like everything else it is valued more when there is a contrast to it. The women's scenes in *Caesar* might with advantage have provided islands of repose in the driving, stirring pattern of the whole.

AN ADMIRABLE CASCA

THE PART OF CASCA is one of Shakespeare's gifts to an actor. Though brief, it has two good scenes, and it is so boldly characterized that it is an immediate favourite with the audience. Among all these subtle, noble Romans, chewing their inexhaustible cud of political scruple, he is refreshingly direct. It was an odd idea of Mr. Langham's to make him a sort of *chamberlain* in the train of Caesar; it was he, armed with an ivory staff, who ordered the procession to the Lupercalia; it was he who directed matters in the Senate-house: this seemed a strange occupation for one who made a point of behaving with as little ceremony as possible. Nevertheless, the device was effective, and gave rather more prominence to Casca than he usually receives.

Douglas Campbell played this part with greater understanding than it often gets, for many actors are so busy making Casca blunt that they have no time or skill left with which to show the mind under the rough exterior. Mr. Campbell's Casca was a very clever man from the first moment he appeared; it was plain that his bluntness was a thin disguise, and in spite of his sniffing, and the strange little picnic which he devoured while talking to Brutus and Cassius, we felt that he missed nothing, and was indifferent to nothing.

It is part of the critic's job to chronicle striking bits of 'business' and feats of skill in the performances he sees; let it be recorded here, then, that while he was describing Caesar's conduct at the Lupercalia, Mr. Campbell threw a raisin high into the air and caught it in his mouth. This trick was curiously effective in making Casca seem like a real Roman, with an existence apart from the action of the play. One saw him immediately as the life of the orgy in many a noble Roman household. The theatre always has a place for such striking effects, and the leap from this bit of clowning to Casca's terror in the scene of the storm, and then to his savagery in the scene of the murder, gave an unusual spread of emotion to a minor role.

CICERO

LEPIDUS

CASCA

LITTER-BEARER

CAESAR

SOOTHSAYER

FLAVIUS

ARTEMIDORUS

MARULLUS

CALPURNIA

BRUTUS

PORTIA

YOUNG CATO

CASSIUS

LUCIUS

A SLAVE

ANTONY

COURTESAN

AGAINST THIS FULLNESS and satisfactory completeness in the smaller parts we must balance a certain flatness in the major ones. It is true that, as Shakespeare draws him, Julius Caesar is not a particularly impressive person. But we may assume, without foisting opinions of our own upon the poet, that Shakespeare expected the legend of Caesar to be present in the minds of his audience. In his day Caesar was as much a character in the popular fancy as Napoleon is—or was until very recently—in our own. Caesar was, after all, one of the Nine Worthies, and unless the cue was clearly given to burlesque them —as is done in *Love's Labour's Lost*—they were objects of respect bordering upon veneration. Mr. Robert Christie gave us a Caesar by no means lacking in dignity; his commanding figure and the splendid resemblance which he had created to the familiar portraits raised us to a high pitch of admiration when he first appeared; but it quickly became apparent that he intended us to accept Caesar as a man haunted by consciousness of his waning powers. Now while this would have been admirable if seconded by some flashes of the mighty conqueror of Rome, it was disturbing by itself. We were given the Caesar who had the falling-sickness, and who was deaf in one ear; we were given a Caesar who laughed unkindly at Calpurnia's dreams, and who boasted like Ancient Pistol of his constancy of character. But where was the mighty Caesar of history?

He was not wholly absent. In the moment of his death Mr. Christie gave us a superb glimpse of a man face to face with his fate; as he reeled from one murderer to another all the eccentricity which had worried us earlier dropped from him, and when he stood at last before Brutus, his face changing from horror and outrage to a stricken acceptance, we saw the great man full and clear. And subsequently, when he made his three ghostly appearances, Caesar was a mighty shadow. Whether this was the actor's conception or the director's it is impossible to guess, and it is not the critic's function to enquire; it must suffice to say that we would have given much for a glimpse of his greatness in the earlier part of the play.

AN AUSTERE ANTONY

As MARK ANTONY, Donald Davis fared best of the leading players, though it cannot be argued that he is thoroughly suited to the role. Although he has no opportunity to show it in this play, Antony is referred to as 'a masquer and a reveller' by Cassius, and we are obviously expected to be conscious of the character he displays in *Antony and Cleopatra*; here again we are brought face to face with the fascination that Roman history had for the Elizabethans, and the knowledge of it that they might be expected to bring to the theatre with them. Now although there are many characters which we are ready to see in Mr. Davis' handsome features, that of a masquer and a reveller is not one of them; the craggy hauteur of his face suggests the rebuker of revels. He made his first entrance, stripped for the games, looking less like a sun-drenched Roman athlete than like Saint Sebastian on his way to the archery butts. But if he could not look like Antony, he was thoroughly capable of acting most of Antony, and the fact that during the year previous to the production he had been appearing regularly in stage plays was of great assistance to him; he did not have to feel his way into the audience's regard—he was able to seize and hold their attention at once. The actor for radio and television lacks this quality of coming to terms immediately with a palpable audience; the assurance that

21

a million people are looking at you in viewers in their homes does not have the same effect on an actor as the plain fact that almost two thousand people are within earshot of your whisper—provided you know how to whisper. Mr. Davis scored heavily because he knew how to deal with an audience at close quarters.

This quality served him best in the Forum scene, precisely where we would have expected it. Mr. Langham set the actor a heavy task, for not only the noise of the Crowd, but its involved and tempestuous movement perpetually distracted our eyes from the apex of the triangle which comprised the stage scene, and at which Antony stood. But again and again this Antony wrested our attention back to himself by gesture, by variety of intonation, and by a considerable degree of that personal magnetism without which no actor can hope to play a leading part. Mr. Davis carried this scene through with fine power and intensity, and when at last the mob dispersed to do its bloody business he changed to a mood of ecstasy in mischief that was one of the thrilling and terrifying things in the play. His cry of—

> Now let it work: mischief, thou art afoot,
> Take thou what course thou wilt.

—combined the glee of the demagogue who has done his work well with a daemonic quality which we are not accustomed to see in Antony. And, immediately following this, his response to the news that Octavius was in Rome—

> He comes upon a wish. Fortune is merry,
> And in this mood will give us anything.

—was not the high spirits of an adventurer and soldier, but rather the secret exultation of a man who feels himself to be in league with fate.

In short, this Antony lacked the full-blooded spirit of the great voluptuary, but it gave us instead a saturnine and astringent quality which had its own high value in the production as a whole. He was, we felt, a fateful member of the triumvirate not so much because of his abilities as a commander as because of his intellectuality. And here he seemed to intrude upon the customary territory of Cassius. Let us hope that some day we shall have an opportunity to see Mr. Davis play Cassius.

A NERVE-WRACKED CASSIUS

IT WAS ONE of the odd pieces of casting in this production that Mr. Lloyd Bochner was chosen to play Cassius. He has many of the qualities which would make him an obvious choice for Antony, a fine voice and a strikingly handsome presence being among them. He is no more able to suggest the voluptuary than Mr. Davis, but he does look convincingly like an athlete. As Cassius, however, he seemed to be determined to show us the nervous irascibility of the man, at whatever expense to the rest of the character. But Cassius is something more than a man with a hot temper; he is a highly successful commander of troops, and a determined and subtle schemer. The Cassius Mr. Bochner gave us lacked weight; one felt that he could never rise to the high command in an army, and when he sought to persuade Brutus to join the conspiracy he gave an effect less of subtlety than of waspishness. In the famous quarrel with Brutus he came close to hysteria and this, combined with Mr. Lorne Greene's lethargy, robbed the scene of most of its value; we were asked to concern ourselves about a quarrel, not between two great men of formidable character, but between a man who would have quarrelled with anybody, and another man who could hardly be roused to quarrel at all. Through most of the play this Cassius was tuned too high for the rest of the company.

He had his moment, however, and it was his last in the play. The weary and disillusioned Cassius, too tired now to be shrill, died as a Roman should, and the picture of him, wreathed and holding the standard in his arms, lingers in the mind.

A SCHOLARLY BRUTUS

BRUTUS, AS SHAKESPEARE HAS DRAWN HIM, harps somewhat monotonously on a single noble string, and here again we must take into account the Elizabethan attitude toward the Romans. The idea still lingered among them that the Roman world was a pinnacle of civilization from which all subsequent history was a decline; the Renaissance had not quite rooted out this medieval concept. And the Elizabethans, like many another people in whom the spirit of boom times was working yeastily—like modern Canadians, for instance—had a passion for ideals of honour and conduct which they could not hope to realize fully in their own lives. Just as many a Canadian seems a little ashamed of his vitality, and yearns for the correct impassivity which he attributes (quite wrongly) to the Victorian Englishman, so the Elizabethans wanted to be as unswervingly virtuous as they conceived the Romans to have been, and were ashamed of their failures. But they liked to see a perfect Roman on the stage, and Brutus probably suited them very well.

He suits us less well, and he is hard to act. Unless the actor brings a great variety of mood, of his own making, to this part, it moves rather heavily, and Mr. Lorne Greene failed in this respect. He was able to give us a Brutus of fine appearance, and the controlled thunder of his voice was very fine in particular passages; but about

24

the performance as a whole there was a monotony which made us feel that, while Brutus was unquestionably noble, honourable and unselfish, he was also a bore.

Mr. Greene has a most unusual voice, a rich and velvety bass which he has under splendid control. But, as every composer of opera either knows, or learns by bitter experience, the lowest notes of a bass voice must be used with the utmost discretion. And that is why the *basso profondo* is less useful than the *basso cantante*; if the singer can carry long passages in his middle range, and even give us a respectable high note or so, he is a very useful fellow, and his splendid bottom register is reserved for moments of the deepest dramatic intensity. But if his low notes are his only good ones, he must not be heard very often, for his single mood is one of solemnity, which may very easily topple over the barrier into absurdity. The late Sir Johnston Forbes-Robertson had a superb voice, with all the thrilling low notes of Mr. Greene: but as we may hear from gramophone records, he used these sparingly and spoke most of the time in an ordinary key; doubtless much of his great reputation as an elocutionist (he was a pupil of Samuel Phelps) was owing to this wise economy. Mr. Greene's capacity as an actor would be more than doubled if he would use the middle register of his voice most of the time, and let us hear his depths only when occasion requires. The low notes are splendid, but it is easy to have too much of them.

The scholarly, reflective side of the character lay well within Mr. Greene's scope, and his soliloquy in the Orchard Scene, and the deliberations with the conspirators which followed it, were moving. His delivery, also, of his speech to the Crowd in the Forum was effective, and for this we must be grateful. Because Brutus' speech is formally rhetorical, and proves in the end to have been less effective than Antony's impassioned harangue, directors sometimes pay little attention to it, and actors give it coldly. Mr. Langham and Mr. Greene knew a trick worth two of that. Brutus' speech was given with full effect; it is a very fine speech, and the Crowd responded to it as such. This had the effect of making their subsequent reversal of sympathy all the more striking; we felt strongly that Antony had a great task in hand when he set out to win them to his side, and when he said:

I am no orator, as Brutus is

we knew that he was speaking simple truth, for Brutus was clearly a great and moving orator. It was in the later scenes, when Brutus becomes a soldier, that Mr. Greene disappointed us, for he did not sufficiently shake off the removed and deliberative manner which had made him so convincing in the earlier passages of the play.

MASTERLY CROWD SCENES

THIS BRINGS US TO THE LAST of the major elements in the production, the Crowd. Mr. Langham had splendid forces at his command, and he marshalled them with great skill. Crowds are rather a new element in theatrical production; there are few records of particularly striking crowd effects in the theatre earlier than the remarkable company which the Duke of Saxe-Meiningen established in 1874, and within which he and his director, Ludwig Chronegk, worked out many of the principles of ensemble which are taken for granted in all theatres today. The old custom seems to have been for the crowds to be recruited by the stage manager, and instructed to keep out of the way of the principal actors, and cheer when given a signal by a leader. But the royal director and Chronegk reformed all that, and prepared elaborate choreographic plans which drew the crowd into the play as a vital part of the action. It is worthy of note that *Julius Caesar* was one of the Meiningen triumphs.

We may assume that the Elizabethan theatre never saw anything like the performance of the Crowd at Stratford. They ranged over the theatre until the stage seemed to include the whole of the auditorium. They appeared sometimes as a mass of forty that looked like four hundred, and sometimes in twos and threes. They were sometimes dull-witted plebs, understanding little of what was said to them, and sometimes they were possessed by demons of malice and fury. In the scene of the death of Cinna the Poet, which is such a startling coda to the scene in the Forum, we saw them seize the unfortunate reveller (brilliantly played by William Hutt) and literally tear him to pieces, so that limbs and a head were flung into the darkness, and only a litter of horrifying scraps was left. In the scene of Caesar's murder this same excitement prevailed; there were enough Senators not implicated in the murder upon the stage to give us the full weight of horror when the dictator was killed. As he reeled from one of his slayers to another, his scarlet mantle seeming transformed into the blood that was being shed, we were concerned not only with him and the men about him, but with the stricken few who were witnesses, and who at last fled shrieking from the place. And in the battles, choreographic though their arrangement was—symbolic battles—we felt no insufficiency, no lack of numbers, no sense of a task half understood and perfunctorily performed.

The director who attempts this sort of thing runs the risk of doing too much, and there were times when we wished that the Crowd would be still, and let us see and hear the chief actors. There were some disturbing confusions, also, between symbolism and realism, as when Caesar died without shedding a drop of blood, and the mantle which Antony showed to the Crowd was realistically stained: we wondered, too, why Caesar who was an uncommonly big man as a living creature and a ghost, went to his funeral in a coffin which might have held a spaniel, but nothing bigger. Apparently there were changes of direction in the course of production which were not fully carried through. But it is pleasanter work to have to complain of faults of imaginative generosity in a production, rather than to regret that too little was done to illuminate the play. The harshest thing that can be said of this production is that Mr. Langham is not yet fully in control of his very great gifts, and it is a happy augury for a young artist when imagination outruns technique.

DURING THE NINE WEEKS' duration of the Festival this production improved strikingly. The crowd scenes lost their strenuosity but not their energy and gained greatly in effectiveness thereby. The performances of the four principal characters emerged more decisively from the pattern of the play; Brutus gained in energy, Caesar in dignity, Cassius in authority, and Mark Antony in that gaiety which he had so sadly lacked. A few scenes had been re-shaped by the director and all of these, and that of the death of Cinna the Poet in particular, were improved by these afterthoughts. . . . The remark made earlier in this criticism that Caesar's coffin was too small must be retracted. I am assured that an adult male, though not a large one, can lie down in it. . . . There was still no general decision as to how to pronounce the Roman names, and it was objectionable to hear Pompey called 'Pom-pay'; in Shakespearean productions it is a good general rule to pronounce Latin as Shakespeare himself pronounced it—that is, as if it were English, and without reference to the style which has come into use during the last thirty years. Upon the whole this production bore out the common stage belief that tragedies improve with repeated performance, while comedies are apt to lose their edge if not frequently re-rehearsed.

KING OEDIPUS

By ROBERTSON DAVIES

KING OEDIPUS

by SOPHOCLES

in a version by W. B. Yeats

OEDIPUS	Douglas Campbell
PRIEST	Eric House
CREON	Robert Goodier
TIRESIAS	Donald Davis
JOCASTA	Eleanor Stuart
MAN FROM CORINTH	Tony van Bridge
OLD SHEPHERD	Eric House
CHORUS LEADER	William Hutt

CHORUS: Roland Bull, Robert Christie, Ted Follows, David Gardner, Bruno Gerussi, Peter Haworth, John Hayes, Roland Hewgill, Edward Holmes, James Manser, Grant Reddick, William Shatner, Bruce Swerdfager, Neil Vipond.

NURSE	Gertrude Tyas
ISMENE AND ANTIGONE	Nomi Cameron and Barbara Franklin

ATTENDANTS ON CREON: Orest Ulan, Bev Wilson, Peter Henderson, John Horton, Harry McGirt, Julian Flett.

SUPPLIANTS: Aimé Aunapuu, Guy Belanger, Nomi Cameron, William Cole, Barbara Franklin, Pauline Galbraith, Robin Gammell, John Gardiner, Robert Gibson, Margaret Griffin, Richard Howard, Charles Jolliffe, Roberta Kinnon, Irene Moszewska, Alex de Naszody, Louis Negin, Ken Pauli, Peter Perehinczuk, Thurston Smith, Gertrude Tyas, Russell Waller, Joan Watts, Alan Wilkinson, Lynn Wilson, Allan Zielonka.

The action of the play takes place in Thebes outside the palace of King Oedipus.

DIRECTED BY TYRONE GUTHRIE
DESIGNED BY TANYA MOISEIWITSCH
MUSIC BY CEDRIC THORPE DAVIE

Masks designed by Tanya Moiseiwitsch and Jacqueline Cundall

KING OEDIPUS, Yeats' version of Sophocles' tragedy, was first produced in the Stratford Festival by Tyrone Guthrie in 1954, and was discussed at length in a book devoted to that season. In considering this revival, therefore, it will suffice to mention the ways in which the 1955 performance differed from the earlier one. It was natural enough to go to the play expecting a different performance of the principal role, possessing its own excellence in contrast to the memorable performance of James Mason the year before. Instead of which we found that the whole production had taken a forward step. Considering how good it had been in 1954, this was a surprise indeed; to have kept to the earlier high standard would have been achievement enough.

A RIPENED PRODUCTION

THEATRICAL PERFORMANCES of the highest order can ripen, however, and this year's *Oedipus* showed, in every respect, the result of a year's pondering on the great play by the director and the players. This is not a type of improvement which surprises us greatly when we observe it in individual performances. Many of us know, within our own play-going experience, conceptions of Hamlet by gifted actors which have grown with the years. The Hamlet which the young actor plays, when first he achieves the status of a leading man, is not the same Hamlet that we see ten years later, when he is famous. And it is not improbable that he will give us an even better Hamlet later on, just before he judges himself too old for the part. Hamlet has been in the depths of his mind for perhaps twenty-five years, his understanding

33

of it growing with his own artistic growth, and his performance improving with his increased technical command. But it is unusual for a whole great production to grow, and in my own experience I have seen only one example of a production which had ripened with years; that was the Habima Theatre's production of *The Dybbuk*; what I saw in 1938 was what Vakhtangov had directed in 1922, and while it would be dishonest of me to claim too complete an understanding of a play acted in Hebrew, it was possessed of a greatness of ensemble which I have never seen equalled. But after that experience, in this matter of ensemble playing, I must rank the Stratford *Oedipus*, and if the company can keep this production in its repertoire, and keep enough of its original actors, it will surely have a world-famous production in the course of a few years. The spirit which animates the Habima is not a spirit known as yet in the theatre anywhere on this continent, but it is just possible that it might be fostered at Stratford.

It is not easy to analyze all the elements in which the production was improved, though some were clearly recognizable. This year the part of the Man from Corinth was played by Tony van Bridge, and played better than Douglas Campbell played it last year. He was more submissive, and less pleased with himself; his personality was more in keeping with his humble station in life, for in these Greek plays it is important that every man should remember his place and not assert himself beyond his rights. The part of the Old Shepherd, played this year by Eric House, was more effective than the same part when William Needles played it; this Shepherd was less pitying, and more pitiful; he was a gentle, confused little creature, utterly overwhelmed by the turn of fate which had brought him into the presence of a distracted king. Physically, also, he was able to bring a touching quality to the part which was valuable; he was so small a thing to give such terrible news.

THE SEER AND THE BIRDS

THERE WERE ALTERATIONS in the production itself which were improvements. More stress was laid on the relationship between Tiresias and the birds from whom he received his dark wisdom. The figure was bird-like, as before, and the necklace of broken egg-shells was the same, but there was some new movement, strongly suggestive of a limping fowl, and when the prophet fell in his cataleptic trance he whirred in his throat, croaked in ecstasy and was indeed alarmingly bird-like. The choreography of his scene had been changed, too, so that the evidence of his blindness was more terrible than it had been before. Nobody knows better than Tyrone Guthrie how to strike terror into the heart of an audience by a display of physical infirmity, and the contrast between the seer's physical darkness and his inner illumination was underlined again and again.

THE PURIFICATION

THE DIFFICULT PASSAGE between Oedipus and his daughters, after the climax of the tragedy, was greatly clarified. As he stands in his scarlet robe, with the two small figures writhing about him, we now see that they are symbolically washing in his blood, and that this is a purification ritual. Whether this can be justified on grounds of scholarship is for scholars to decide; it justifies itself amply in theatrical terms, for unless something of this kind is used to illuminate this section of the play, it is apt to lose the sympathy of a modern audience. When a play is consid-

35

erably over 2000 years old it is impossible for an audience to respond to it precisely as its first auditors did, however great and universal its theme may be. The part of *Oedipus* which immediately follows the last entrance of the blinded king undoubtedly had significance for the Greeks which it has lost for us, and the method of dealing with it in this production offers, in unmistakable terms, a possible solution which is congruous with the play, and deeply moving.

CHORUS AND RITUAL

OF THE FOURTEEN MEN who comprised the Chorus, ten had been in it last year, and the Chorus Leader, William Hutt, was the same. Thus, in this extremely important area of the play there was a continuity of experience, and a deepening of interpretation which brought new quality to the performance. The Chorus of a Greek tragedy is not, or should not be, a verse-speaking choir, reciting comment on the action; approached in that way there would be no chance that the Chorus could improve as this one had done. The Chorus is the link between the audience and the principal actors; if we accept Dr. Guthrie's ritualistic concept of drama, the Chorus are the intermediaries between the worshippers and the priests. In a play like *Oedipus* they give voice to the thoughts of the audience with an eloquence and cogency which the audience could not hope to summon up for itself. In the 1955 production the Chorus seemed closer to the audience, and more eloquent in expression, than it had been in 1954.

Some of this change was brought about by altered movement. The use of the stage by the Chorus this year was freer than it had been before, and the groupings, though complex and dictated by consideration for the decorative effect on the stage, all appeared perfectly natural and inevitable. No one who has not tried it can understand how difficult this sort of stage management can be. To transmute formal verse and formal action into a pattern of movement which unites and supplements them both requires theatre genius of the highest order. What we saw was, in effect, a stately dance and perhaps as near to dancing as we could accept in a performance of a Greek play. Modern theatre audiences think of serious dancing chiefly in terms of formal ballet; what sort of dancing was done by the Chorus in a Greek play is imperfectly known, and in our age we have no style of dancing which can be successfully combined with poetic speech.

The Greek Choruses danced and sang, and until some striking advance is made in the technique of opera we shall not recapture that effect, which must undoubtedly have been deeply moving and exalting. But the Chorus in *Oedipus* moved in this direction; they were close to dance, and close to song, and their actual passage of song was even more touching than it was in 1954. Once again, for anything comparable, I must recur to the technique of Habima, where speech and movement rise by imperceptible stages to song and dance, and drop equally imperceptibly to less exalted levels. The lyric quality, which is so rarely encountered in the theatre, and which we experience under so many disabilities in opera, was truly present in this production, and its effect was magical.

A STRONG OEDIPUS

MUCH OF THE INTEREST in this season's production of *King Oedipus* arose, naturally, from the contrast between James Mason's performance and that of Douglas Campbell. I have praised Mr. Mason highly and sincerely, and

I do not feel that it detracts from his fine performance to say that Douglas Campbell was able to give us more of Oedipus. And the reason for this was in a great measure a matter of physique.

Because actors are artists who appear before us to very great intellectual advantage, we sometimes fall into the error of thinking of them primarily as people of intellect. Of course they bring intelligence of a very special sort to their work, but it is not unkind to point out that an actor is not primarily relying on his own intellect when Shakespeare or Sophocles provides what he has to say. The actor must have a good voice and the intelligence to say what he has to say with effect. But if he aspires to be an actor of classic roles he must possess either a great physique or he must be very skilful in making up for the lack of one. Everybody knows that singing an important role in opera is hard work. But we sometimes forget that acting a great role in a play is as hard, or harder, and that strength and physical training are invaluable assets. An actor is an interpretative rather than a creative artist, and important as intellect is, technique is more important still.

Mr. Campbell is a good example of the well-graced actor. He has a fine tenor voice with a big range, and he has developed it by singing. He is heavily built, and muscular. He is a dancer. He is a fencer. In boxing terms, he is a heavyweight where Mr. Mason is a middleweight. Consequently he was able to make light of the heavy harness which goes with the role of Oedipus. He wore the great mask as though it were his own head; he moved easily in the heavy robes; he could walk swiftly —even to the point of running—on the high *cothurnoi*. Where Mr. Mason achieved effects by repose and silence, Mr. Campbell topped them by heroic movement and sound.

38

It is a great pleasure to watch a subtle actor hinting at mighty things; we admire the skill of such a player as, for instance, the late George Arliss, who by a trick of the eye, a hesitation in the voice, or the turn of a hand, created finely dramatic effects. Such acting is of a high order; it is to this school that Irving belonged. But we can weary of subtlety, and yearn for direct action; it is a joy to see an actor who does not suggest an effect, but gives it to us at full strength, sweeping us up in a whirlwind of passion. Mr. Campbell belongs in this class.

In his great speech describing his encounter with Laius, for instance, this Oedipus acted the whole scene for us superbly; with voice and gesture, and splendid use of the mask, he made us see the battle at the crossway, when the angry old man struck at the young wayfarer, and was himself stricken to the earth. The great head tossed; the more than human arms swept through the air, and for the instant we were caught up in a battle of demigods.

At a later point in the play, when the suspicion of his fate becomes intolerable, this Oedipus dropped to the floor and crawled to Jocasta, who stooped to comfort him. This was a splendid conception, for which of us ever expected to see that huge figure take the posture of a child? But Mr. Campbell, in his performance, looked far below the surface of Oedipus and gave us not only the tragedy of a king, but one of the deep primal tragedies of man.

We go to performances of plays like *King Oedipus* with so many expectations and associations of our own that we are always in danger of seeing in the performance something that is not there. But is this, in every case, a danger? Is not a fine performance by an actor capable, within reason, of being understood in many different ways? I have long felt that, at the beginning of the play, Oedipus has, very deep in his mind, some uneasy feeling that he is the great sinner who has brought the plague upon Thebes; and as the play progresses this feeling mounts from the depths of his mind to its surface, as ancient memories and their associations are stirred. If we take the plot simply as the story of a man who discovers a terrible truth about himself it is striking in its effect, but we cannot escape a feeling that Oedipus was uncommonly stupid not to have reached his conclusions before he did: but if we take the tragedy as the gradual uncovering of something which a man has refused to recognize in himself, all his reluctance and resistance to the truth seems human and pitiable. It appeared to me, at least, that this was the way in which Douglas Campbell understood the part and played it.

We saw him from the first as both a great king and a man strangely troubled; yet he trusted to his luck, and appealed to it wildly; it was unthinkable to him that the misery he dimly suspected could be his, and yet the suspicion would not be still; and so, when the conclusion could no longer be escaped, he suffered the misery not of a man struck down by an unexpected blow, but a man who falls prey to an enemy of whose approach he has long and uneasily been conscious. This was a fine and subtle conception of Oedipus, carried out in terms of classic acting of the most robust and forthright kind.

To contrast Mr. Mason and Mr. Campbell once again, the former gave us a performance of Oedipus which was illuminating in the sense that a very fine reading of the play might be so; he aroused much feeling in us of an intellectual nature, and we pitied the great king's suffering. But Mr. Campbell extended our boundaries of feeling; he made us suffer, not intellectually, but physically and emotionally; we were able to identify ourselves with him more readily and completely than with Mr. Mason. Both conceptions of the part were coherent and

40

complete, but Mr. Campbell was much better equipped as an actor to impose his conception upon us; his physical and intellectual energy could not be resisted, and we were drawn into the play more deeply than in 1954.

It is a point of interest to those who study the technique of acting that Mr. Campbell's vigorous performance seemed to make it possible for the rest of the company to act much more freely and eloquently than they did a year earlier. Experience may account for some of this, but not for all of it. They, like the audience, drew heavily upon his strength and were given a greater degree of confidence by it.

If a musical similitude is permissible, Mr. Campbell played Oedipus in a major key, Mr. Mason in a minor key. Both had their special excellence, but with a great play it is not a question of what the actor can make of it, but what it will make of him. For the majesty of Sophocles, Mr. Campbell was the more eloquent instrument.

GUTHRIE AND TRAGEDY

IT HAS SOMETIMES BEEN SAID in criticism of Dr. Guthrie that he is not at his best directing tragedy. Such a judgement will not stand examination in the light of this production of *King Oedipus*. Dr. Guthrie has a great talent for comedy, and particularly for that aspect of comedy which deals in the grotesque and the farouche. But it is not nature's way to make a man great in comedy without giving him some comparable weight on the other side; it is impossible to comprehend great comedy without some strong feeling for tragedy. Dr. Guthrie has not always been happy in his treatment of those tragedies which spring from the sources of romantic love, but this same aspect of life frequently eludes him in comedy. In comedy, however, it is easier to avoid the issue. But in such a tragedy as *King Oedipus* we face one of the acknowledged great creations of the poetic spirit, and Dr. Guthrie has given us a great realization of it on the stage. No man comprehends all things even in the realm of a single art, but a man who can conceive and bring forth an *Oedipus* on this scale cannot be denied the stature of a great director of tragedy.

THIS PRODUCTION did not improve as the Festival progressed, the falling-off being noticeable in the case of the Chorus, whose speaking lost much of its eloquence. Where, in the early performances and in the 1954 production, we had heard good clear speaking, unmarked by any regional accent, we now heard intrusive Canadian r's and flat a's, which robbed the verse of dignity and music. If this play is to stay in the repertory, it will obviously have to be re-rehearsed frequently.

Criticism which was offered in *Twice Have the Trumpets Sounded* of the Yeats translation of the play is given some support by the information recently imparted to me by a Greek scholar that Yeats was not himself proficient in Greek, and prepared his translation from several existing English versions. While this does not mean that his version is not in very fine English of its kind, it seems to dispel any notion that *King Oedipus* is the product of one great poetic intelligence working directly upon another. It suggests even more clearly that Yeats prepared his version for a small group performing the play in humble circumstances.

In spite of some falling-off in performance as the Festival progressed, I am content to repeat a judgement offered in another place: we may see better productions of *Oedipus* in our time, but we should be fools to count on it.

THE MERCHANT OF VENICE

By ROBERTSON DAVIES

THE MERCHANT OF VENICE
By WILLIAM SHAKESPEARE

ANTONIO	Robert Goodier
SALARINO	Edward Holmes
SALANIO	Lloyd Bochner
ANTONIO'S SERVANT	Peter Haworth
BASSANIO	Donald Harron
LORENZO	Neil Vipond
GRATIANO	William Shatner
PORTIA	Frances Hyland
NERISSA	Helen Burns
BALTHASAR	Bruce Swerdfager
STEPHANO	Roland Bull
SHYLOCK	Frederick Valk
THE PRINCE OF MOROCCO	Lorne Greene
LAUNCELOT GOBBO	Ted Follows
OLD GOBBO	William Hutt
LEONARDO	Grant Reddick
JESSICA	Charlotte Schrager
THE PRINCE OF ARRAGON	Eric House
TUTORS	John Hayes, Russell Waller, Roland Hewgill
MAIDS: Gold	Pauline Galbraith
Silver	Lynn Wilson
Lead	Joan Watts
TUBAL	Bruno Gerussi
THE DUKE OF VENICE	Robert Christie

SERVANTS, MASQUERS, MEN-AT-ARMS, MAGNIFICOES: Guy Belanger, Tony van Bridge, Nomi Cameron, William Cole, Julian Flett, Barbara Franklin, Robin Gammell, John Gardiner, David Gardner, Robert Gibson, Margaret Griffin, Peter Henderson, Richard Howard, Charles Jolliffe, Jim Manser, Harry McGirt, Alex de Naszody, Louis Negin, Peter Perehinczuk, Thurston Smith, Orest Ulan, Beverley Wilson, Alan Wilkinson, Allan Zielonka.

CHORISTERS: Helen Baumbach, Audrey Conroy, Eileen Hunter, Jean Moorehead, Miriam Root, Velda Scott, John Boyden, Lloyd Bradshaw, Keith Elliott, Gordon Scott.

The action takes place in Venice and at Belmont.

DIRECTED BY TYRONE GUTHRIE
DESIGNED BY TANYA MOISEIWITSCH
MUSIC BY JOHN COOK

HERE WE HAVE A FAIRY-TALE, told by a supreme poet of the theatre who is also a master of stage effect. Surely this is a great matter; but there are many people who profess to see something different, and in their opinion greater, in *The Merchant of Venice* than this. We have all of us a tendency to create private Shakespeares in our own image, and people who are not very susceptible to fantasy, and take great pleasure in what they choose to regard as profundity, have found their own sort of profundity in this play. They invest it with the wrong kind of seriousness. It is serious in the sense that Mozart's operas are serious, but they try to find in it the seriousness which is proper to Ibsen.

We are constantly being reminded that Shakespeare was not for an age, but for all time; if we insist too literally on this aspect of his universality we soon find ourselves in difficulties. He was very much a man of his time, and in *The Merchant of Venice* he was writing for his time, without a thought for us. He wrote for a theatre which was not so heavily burdened with intellectuality as ours; he wrote plays for audiences to accept and enjoy as they watched them, and some of the perplexing passages in his plays seem to arise from his desire to rouse his audience to enthusiasm simply to provide a splendid theatrical effect. As we watch this play, we must live in the moment; we must ride the surf of the action, enjoying each wave as it comes, until we are gently deposited on the beach. If we are incapable of this sort of enjoyment we shall never understand this comedy.

TRUTH IN A FAIRY-TALE

IF WE TRY TO UNDERSTAND the play in realistic terms we shall be in trouble at once. The Tale of the Caskets is

47

manifestly ridiculous. What father would leave such a will? What suitor with enough sense to come in out of the rain would dream of choosing any other than the leaden casket? There is no truth to be found on the surface of this plot. All its truth lies in the fairy-tale quality of the story, in which the Prince will inevitably win the Princess by solving the riddle which holds her in thrall. Portia's father still speaks through the caskets; he still chooses his daughter's husband by imposing a trial of wisdom, or cunning, upon all comers. This is more than a Renaissance tale; it is one of the primal stories in which all nations, at all times, have delighted.

The Tale of the Pound of Flesh is equally unsuitable for realistic discussion. Why a pound? Why not ask for Antonio's heart, and make sure of his death? Would anyone die because a pound of flesh were cut from him? And why does Shylock's refusal to provide a physician in the court appear as such a heinous matter? If we are dealing in realism, there is nothing whatever to prevent Bassanio, or the Duke, from calling in a dozen physicians. But in a fairy-tale the darkling menace of the villain springs from sources far below these realistic considerations, and it can only be conquered by magical intervention. Portia provides that element; her law is not impressive, but her good magic which defeats the bad magic of Shylock stirs a response in all of us who are not wholly dead to the appeal of magic.

Similarly the supposition that Bassanio and Gratiano could meet their wives in the court and not recognize them is nonsense if we take it realistically. This is part of the light-hearted convention of a sort of fiction which rises high above the details of realism; it belongs to a world where a cloak or a hat provides an impenetrable disguise. There are people who say that this is the world of childhood, but I question their wisdom; it is a world which children inhabit, certainly, and which they understand in a childlike way, but it is also a world to which many adults never forget the road, and which grows more splendid to them every day they live; it is that world of the imagination from which virtually all beauty springs.

THE UNSELFCONSCIOUS ARTIST

BUT IF THIS PLAY must be related to the world of fantasy, you may say, how comes it that we find so many passages in it which are clearly applicable to the life of every day? Why is it not all flyaway stuff like, for example, Rostand's *Les Romanesques*? Surely the answer is that Shakespeare was to a great extent an unselfconscious artist; he did not write to a theory or a pattern; we produce these to explain him, but he had no truck with such things. He wrote to please his audience and himself, and like every master of fantasy in literature he was likely to load it with any fine thing that came into his mind. It is the inextricable mixture of fantasy and strong poetic insight (which is the best kind of realism) which makes this a great play; it is also the quality which makes people who like realism better than fantasy try to understand it all in realistic terms. The process is like removing the bubbles from champagne in the hope of producing a wholesome temperance beverage.

Portia and Bassanio must be considered as an Enchanted Princess and her Questing Prince, or they become rather unpleasant young people. She becomes a very rich girl with a talent for logic-chopping which would be the ruin of any marriage; he becomes a fortune-hunter who asks a friend to stake him to a final chance to catch a rich wife. But if we have any feeling for poetry at all, we cannot reduce them to these terms; the very existence of Nerissa and Gratiano forbids it. Their comic reduplication of the romance of the Prince and Princess is of an operatic simplicity; unless your soprano and tenor are provided with contralto and baritone counterparts, what sort of ensemble can you contrive? And if we take these romances in dull earnest, what are we to make of the affair of Jessica and her Lorenzo? We must feel that the girl is right to run away from her father, and steal his money, and we can only feel this if we accept her as the daughter of a wicked magician who steals some of his magic power. If she is a real Jewess who deserts her father and her faith for a young man with a talent for rhapsodizing about the stars, she is an unprincipled girl who deserves to come to a bad end.

But in considering the play as poetic fantasy, we run into difficulties when we appraise the character of Shylock. He is no flat villain, like Barabas in Marlowe's *Jew of Malta*. He is a strongly-realized, human character who comes near to breaking the play. It is the extraordinary power with which Shakespeare has invested Shylock, more than any other consideration, which has led scholars and actors to take *The Merchant of Venice* as a realistic picture of life. Yet, for reasons which have already been mentioned, we cannot accept Shylock as photographically real; he is credited with a power in the play which would have been utterly impossible for any Venetian or Renaissance Jew to wield. The place he occupies is that of the wicked magician in the fairy-tale—the powerful menace to goodness and happiness which can only be defeated by a decisive and unforeseen stroke of a magic greater than his own.

SHYLOCK IS AN EXTREMELY ATTRACTIVE ROLE and it has
been played in many different ways. There is a persistent
tradition that it was once played as a comedy part, and
that it was thus that Shakespeare intended it. Nobody
with much knowledge of Shakespeare could believe anything of the sort. But it is true that there was a comic
Shylock in a play called *The Jew of Venice*, written by
Lord Lansdowne, and performed first in 1701. This
comment on it from *Biographia Dramatica, or A Com-
panion to The Playhouse* (published in 1764), gives us a
notion of its quality:

> This play is altered from Shakespeare's *Merchant
> of Venice*, and in some respects with judgement.
> The introduction of the feast, more particularly
> where the Jew is placed at a separate table, and
> drinks to his money as his only mistress, is a
> happy thought; yet, on the whole, his Lordship
> has greatly lessened both the beauty and effect
> of the original; which, notwithstanding this
> modernized piece, aided by magnificence and
> music, still stands its ground, and will ever con-
> tinue one of the darling representations of the
> theatre. . . . In this play, as Rowe remarks, the
> character of Shylock (which was performed by
> Dogget) is made comic, and we are prompted to
> laughter instead of detestation.

Dogget was a famous low comedian, and he played
Shylock in Lansdowne's play in a red wig; but I can find
no record of Shakespeare's play having been performed
with a comic Shylock—though I was solemnly taught
when I was a schoolboy that this was so, and that we were
very clever people to have discovered that Shakespeare
might secretly have meant him to be serious.

That detestation which the eighteenth century writer
mentions has sometimes been as remote from popular

taste as the idea of a comic Shylock is to us. During the nineteenth century several eminent actors played Shylock as a man desperately wronged, and driven almost to madness. The greatest of these, Sir Henry Irving, created a Shylock so aristocratic of demeanour, and so distinguished of intellect, that the play became his personal tragedy. He did not, however, go so far as some earlier players, who finished the play at the end of the Trial Scene, concluding that when Shylock had made his final exit there was nothing of any consequence to follow. For at least a century this was Shylock's play. It is only in comparatively recent times that the balance of the plot has been rediscovered, and the fairy-tale nature of the whole piece brought forward, and for this, as for so many other illuminations of Shakespeare, we are indebted to the late Harley Granville-Barker.

NOT AN ANTI-SEMITIC PLAY

FOR OBVIOUS REASONS the play has always been offensive to some Jews, and within our own time Jewish groups have made protestations against its public performance. The Stratford presentation was the subject of some criticism of this kind. Such a book as this is not the place to discuss this issue in detail, but it may be said that such protests constitute a form of censorship which would remove a dramatic masterwork from the popular repertoire. Censorship of any kind, once it is countenanced, is extremely difficult to control. While we must sympathize with the racial sensibility of a people which has been often and cruelly abused, it is impossible for a student of Shakespeare's work to regard the character of Shylock as an attack on Jews in general, or to believe that *The Merchant of Venice* would lead anyone down the crooked path of anti-Semitism.

Matters of religion, however, are notoriously treacherous ground for dispute. Mr. Nevill Coghill has asserted that when Antonio makes the condition that Shylock must become a Christian he is 'instantly [offering] him (so far as it is in the power of a human being to do so) the eternal life that is his own best jewel'. Considering the conditions under which the jewel is offered, we may think with equal justification that Antonio is having one more humiliating kick at his old enemy. The behaviour of the Christians in this play is certainly nothing for a true Christian to exult over, and if we were to take *The*

SALARINO

Merchant of Venice as a realistic depiction of life it is quite as bitterly anti-Christian as it is anti-Jewish.

THE CAUSE OF ANTONIO'S SADNESS

THE STATE OF THE WORLD in our time has given the character of Shylock an importance which is not inherent in it as an element in the play. But the Stratford production put stress on another element in the piece which has been much neglected. It is called *The Merchant of Venice,* and the Merchant is Antonio. Yet we have been accustomed to seeing the play performed in such a way that Antonio was a rather dull character of

53

SALANIO

secondary interest. Dr. Guthrie has chosen to emphasize the very warm friendship which exists between Antonio and Bassanio, bringing it forward as a homosexual romance. But if this attitude toward the play gains favour, and the growing interest in, and sympathy for, the plight of homosexuals increases, our grandchildren may see the day when well-organized groups of homosexuals protest against the presentation of the play because it shows one of their number heartlessly betrayed by a young man for whom he has undergone the utmost danger.

The revelation of this theme in the play may give offence in some quarters, but it cannot easily be argued down. Even so careful and sober a scholar as the late Sir Edmund Chambers has drawn attention to it. Once again we must bear in mind that this play was written primarily for the Renaissance world and not for our own, and that in that world, with its attachment to Greek ideals of life, homosexuality was not held in horror. And nowadays people who have had opportunities to see something of life under varied circumstances know that homosexual love is by no means uncommon, and that it is no more necessarily gross or degrading than romantic love between men and women. The homosexual is quite as often a courageous, intelligent and admirable person as his heterosexual brother, and it is his personal character, rather than his sexual disposition, which makes his love noble or despicable. We are shown Antonio as a man much respected, and the terms in which his love for Bassanio are made known are restrained. His sadness at the beginning of the play, which puzzles his companions, becomes clear enough when we find that Bassanio wants his help to win Portia. And, in the scene of the Trial, what are we to make of this, his last speech before Shylock exacts his penalty:

54

> I am arm'd and well prepared;
> Give me your hand, Bassanio, fare you well,
> Grieve not that I am fallen to this for you;
> For herein Fortune shows herself more kind
> Than is her custom: it is still her use
> To let the wretched man outlive his wealth,
> To view with hollow eye and wrinkled brow
> An age of poverty; from which lingering penance
> Of such misery doth she cut me off.
> Commend me to your honourable wife,
> Tell her the process of Antonio's end,
> Say how I lov'd you, speak me fair in death;
> And when the tale is told, bid her be judge
> Whether Bassanio had not once a love.

In the Stratford production this element in the play was handled with discretion, but it was unmistakable, and it added greatly to the effect of the whole, for it carried into the lyrical Fifth Act some of the quality of the Trial Scene. To the theme of the Three Caskets and the Pound of Flesh was added a third, fully as powerful as either—a theme of Renunciation. This has always been an attractive element in drama; such popular favourites as *The Only Way* were built on nothing else. When the lovers had left the stage at the end of the play, we saw the lonely figure of Antonio, holding in his hand the letter which tells of the restoration of his fortunes; but he has lost his love, and as the letter drops from his fingers and the lights fade, we feel a bittersweet pang for him which gives the play, on the modern stage, a new and important dimension.

Much has been written about Shakespeare and homosexuality, and the Sonnets have been a battle-ground for sixty years where those who wish to claim him as a homosexual genius contend with those who take a larger view of his nature. There can be no doubt that Shakespeare understood homosexuality, as he understood murder, remorse and romantic love—as well as the ludicrous and repellent aspects of heterosexual love where it has grown rank. *The Merchant of Venice* adds nothing to the arguments on either side, but when the affection of Antonio for Bassanio is given its full weight in the play many things in it are illuminated which had formerly been dark.

SERIOUS BUT NOT SOLEMN

THE STRATFORD PRODUCTION never strayed from the adult's fairy-tale conception of the play; it was like a story from Bandello or Boccaccio richly brought to life. Where the play is serious it was finely serious, but it never substituted mere solemnity for seriousness. Some detailed attention has already been given to the treatment of the Renunciation theme in the play; it was tellingly but delicately stated, and Antonio's affection for Bassanio was in that tradition of the love of an older man for a younger—a love which is at once passionate, and yet paternal and protective—which is familiar in the Greek and the Renaissance world. The theme of the Three Caskets was all in a vein of romantic fantasy. The caskets themselves were objects of beauty, and it was a good moment when the Prince of Arragon took the fool's head from the silver casket, and read its message on a long tongue which pulled out of its mouth like a tape. The theme of the Pound of Flesh was treated as full-blooded melodrama. The first encounter of Antonio and Shylock was marked by a reapportionment of lines which was effective and, unless I am very much deceived, correct. In all printed texts Shylock's speech at this point begins:

> How like a fawning publican he looks!
> I hate him for he is a Christian!

JESSICA

But in this production the first of these lines was given to Antonio, in whose mouth it makes more sense than if it is spoken by Shylock. Why would the proud merchant seem 'fawning', even to his enemy? The tension of this relationship mounted irresistibly to the point in the Trial Scene where Antonio is brought up from the depths of the prison, tied to a hurdle and ready for the knife. There was a splendour of danger about the Trial, right until the moment of Portia's triumph, for in this production she did not arrive full of guileful certainty, and armed with a quibble by her cousin Bellario; she found her solution on the stage, before our eyes, and struck down her opponent almost on the spur of the moment. This is not the kind of thing which commends itself to the realists, and it does not bear close examination in retrospect, but it is a splendidly thrilling stage effect. The play, it must be repeated, is meant to be enjoyed as it progresses, and this was the highest of many pinnacles of excitement.

DELIGHTS FOR THE EYE

THE PRODUCTION, as always when Dr. Guthrie is in charge, was marked by brilliance and delicacy of imagination. We are used to seeing the suitors for Portia sharply differentiated, but not so sharply as here, where the scimitar-flourishing Moor is contrasted with a Prince of Arragon who seemed to be the most obscure and most haemophilic of all the Hapsburgs. The caskets were carried by girls dressed in costumes of golden, silver and leaden hues—Miss Lead being so sadly unequal to her heavy task that she often had to be helped by Portia's servant, Balthasar. During the scene of Jessica's elopement we were given just enough of the atmosphere of a Venetian carnival to suggest the atmosphere of a rich and gay city, but we were never allowed to weary of it. The costumes and the properties were in Miss Tanya Moiseiwitsch's best manner—fanciful, striking but never marred by opulence for its own sake. All the elements of the production were united to suggest, but never to insist upon, the splendour of Venice. The eye was fully satisfied, but never wearied or distracted.

AND THE EAR

THE HEARING, also, was happily ministered to, for as part of Portia's household there was an excellent choir which sang unaccompanied music by John Cook, to supplement the action where it was needed. The music was most effective at two high points in the play. The first of these was when Bassanio made his choice among the caskets; the choir welcomed him, as it had done in the case of the other suitors, but it sang 'Tell Me Where is Fancy Bred' while he took a pause for quiet deliberation. As he stood in the centre of the stage, considering his choice, attendants with crowned and ribboned standards wove in and out among the actors, creating a pattern which was beautiful in itself, and helpful to the action of the play. Dr. Guthrie's productions move at great speed, and sometimes a rest is needed. Bassanio's long pause provided such a moment of rest, and the music was given full opportunity to create an atmosphere of romance.

Similarly in the Fifth Act, during the love scene between Lorenzo and Jessica, we were given enough music to support the lines, but before Portia's entrance we were allowed to hear it for some little time without other sound. It was a splendid device to give us a moment of respite after the excitement of the Trial Scene, to suggest the romantic beauty of the night, and to prepare the stage for one of the most charming of Shakespearean

59

finales. We carried away from this production a sense of having heard music which, without obtruding on the play, had lent its own quality to it, and which had laid its own gentle restraint on the sometimes breathless pace of the action.

GRAPPLING WITH THE GOBBOS

THE PRODUCTION contained a variety of good performances. The Gobbos are among the stumbling-blocks for modern audiences. We have lost the Renaissance relish for this particular type of jocosity; we have our own strange appetites, as an evening with

LAUNCELOT GOBBO

radio or television will show, but the run-of-the-mill, flat-footed foolery of Shakespeare's day is not the run-of-the-mill, flat-footed foolery of our own, and as a general thing we endure Launcelot Gobbo and his father, knowing that they cannot last long. Ted Follows and William Hutt made Canadian rustics of the Gobbos, which gave them some freshness, though no more wit than before. Old Gobbo's hat was a splendid creation, and he provided us with one moment of true pathos when he discovered that his son was not dead. But the scene between father and son is an uncomfortable one for an audience today; we do not think blindness

OLD GOBBO

funny, and we cannot greatly like a son who pretends to be dead in order to make his father weep. Dr. Guthrie is not a man to soften such a scene as this, and he is right not to do so; let us by all means see what a Renaissance English audience considered funny, so long as we are not obliged to think it funny ourselves. Through the remainder of the play Ted Follows did what Launcelot has to do capably, but he has not the true comedian's gift of making bricks without straw.

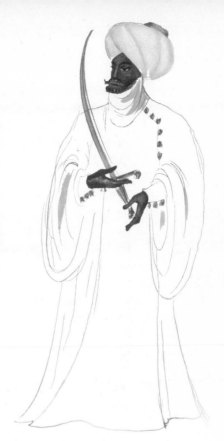

PORTIA'S UNSUCCESSFUL SUITORS

SOME MENTION has already been made of the two suitors who do not win Portia. Lorne Greene was a figure of tawny majesty as the Prince of Morocco and his first entrance was a fine sight, but he was not able to continue at this high pitch, and grew a little dull before he had made his choice. It would have been interesting to see him blacker; no doubt a Moroccan is coffee-coloured, but it is probable that Shakespeare thought of the Prince as a Negro, and a coal-black face under the huge white turban which Miss Moiseiwitsch had decreed would have made a fine effect. But the monotony of voice which betrayed Mr. Greene in

Julius Caesar was apparent in this smaller part, also.

As Eric House played him, the Prince of Arragon was one of the fine creations of the production. Pale, clad in black and shadowed by three Tutors who wore those shovel hats traditionally associated with the Spanish clergy, he was chilling, repellent and yet also pitiable. When he moved, he was a bored procession of one; when he spoke, it was from a body in which the white corpuscles had long taken the upper hand; he touched nothing which was not given to him by one of his clerical keepers; even the three caskets were snatched from their virgin attendants by these Arragonian vultures. Yet there was a true nobility about him. When he found the fool's head in the silver casket it was his Tutors who showed dismay and chagrin, not he. He read its bitter message to the end, and even improvised a few limping lines in the same metre, to show that he, like Bottom, could gleek upon occasion. Prisoner of his great inheritance though he might be, there was a spark of gallantry in this dreadful little prince, and though he was a figure of fun we admired him. To convey so much of a character in a single scene is a considerable achievement.

THE MIGHT OF VENICE

THE COURT OF VENICE must impress more by its dignity than by its intellect; it exists simply to tremble before Shylock, and the grander it is, the more effective the scene. Miss Moiseiwitsch had robed the Magnificoes in several different reds, which suggested that they had all bought their ceremonial robes at different times, like Peers at a Coronation. There were enough of them to make an impressive show, and a background for Robert Christie, who played the Duke. He had chosen to characterize this not very clearly drawn ruler as an eccentric, humming-and-hawing old aristocrat; it was well done, but would not the scene be stronger if the Duke were not quite so realistic, so matter-of-fact? The Duke is the visible sign of the might of Venice, and Shylock sets him at naught; would not a Duke more awesome in his dignity be more useful to the production? There are characters in Shakespeare who are not much more than walking and talking scenery, and the Duke is one of them. To give him too much individual character may be to lessen his effectiveness in the play.

THE SALADS

THERE IS SOME CONFUSION in the texts of this play about the friends of Bassanio and Antonio, known to actors as The Salads. Sometimes they appear simply as Salanio and Salarino, as they did in this production, but occasionally the first of the two is called Solanio, and now and then an intruder named Salerio finds his way into the text. The late Stephen Leacock claimed to have known a man who discovered a Saloonio in this play. It is not of much consequence, for they are ungrateful parts, designed chiefly to 'feed' cues to more important characters. And, as Salarino, that is what Edward Holmes did, though not always accurately. But as Salanio, Lloyd Bochner provided a surprise in Act Two, in the scene in which he describes Shylock's rage and despair when he finds that his daughter has fled. There was a bitterness of mockery in this which was startling, and extremely valuable to the play, for it gave us a strong sense of the enmity that Shylock had incurred, and of the storm that was brewing. The venom of the Christians' hatred of the infidel was strongly accented in this production, and here we were given one of its most shocking manifestations. Once again we were reminded that Stratford's

repertory system enables producers to cast powerful actors in comparatively minor roles.

ANTONIO REVEALED

THE CONCEPTION of the role of Antonio, the Merchant of the title, which brought a new quality to this production, has already been discussed. The part was played by Robert Goodier with dignity and restraint. His sadness was not a matter of sighs and gloomy looks, contrasting with the light-heartedness of his companions; it was an inner quality, which he seemed at pains to conceal. He played Antonio,

SHYLOCK

indeed, very much in the manner of Sidney Carton, which was precisely the right note to hit. In many productions Antonio seems to be a nuisance in the Fifth Act; he is a stranger and he is in low spirits, even though he has escaped death and has recovered his fortunes; unless we see him as a deserted lover his melancholy in the last act of the play is hard to excuse. But it was in that light that we saw him at Stratford, and his melancholy gave an agreeably sombre contrast to the high spirits of the three pairs of lovers. And as he was the last figure that we saw on the stage, the play closed,

ANTONIO

not with Gratiano's racy joke about guarding Nerissa's ring, but with the melancholy man whom we had seen when the play began, and thus Antonio's misfortune bracketed the whole of the action. Many playgoers, who had seen *The Merchant of Venice* many times, must have felt, as I did, that they had seen Antonio for the first time.

VENUSTAS, ET PRAETEREA NIHIL

THE LOVE STORY of Lorenzo and Jessica is to that of Bassanio and Portia as the moon is to the sun. Their situation is strongly romantic, and they have one of the great lyric scenes of the play. But to persuade the audience to accept them it is not enough to put two handsome young people into the roles, and hope that all will be well. To create an atmosphere of romance is one of the most difficult tasks that can be required of an actor or an actress; it demands a technique so difficult and so fine that very few people acquire it until they are considerably past the age of the characters they are called on to play. A director has his choice: he can give such parts to players who have youth and beauty of precisely the type that is wanted, and hope that the audience will forgive some lightweight acting; or he can find players who are fully capable of extracting the last ounce of romantic beauty from the lines, but whose appearance is no longer dewy. Dr. Guthrie chose the former course, and cast Neil Vipond and Charlotte Schrager as Lorenzo and Jessica.

Their appearance was in every way suitable, and Miss Schrager has just the type of beauty for the semi-Oriental dress which Miss Moiseiwitsch gave her. But neither was fully audible, and neither was skilled in speaking poetry. To do this it is not enough to look poetic and feel poetic;

it is necessary to be able to understand the poetry thoroughly and to have a technique by which that understanding can be conveyed to a large audience. Mr. Vipond and Miss Schrager cannot justly be blamed because they lack such a technique; it takes years to acquire it. Therefore, though they made a gallant attack upon their roles, they cannot be said to have succeeded in them. It was not that they failed the play; it was simply that they did not understand the degree of intensity with which the other actors were performing. And for this reason they came to us faintly, and rather charmingly, like music heard intermittently across a lake on a summer evening. But much could be forgiven them because of their appearance.

MASCULINITY WITHOUT MANLYDOM

WITH GRATIANO AND NERISSA we felt no such lack of vigour. William Shatner is one of the most promising of the younger actors at Stratford; he has zest and attack, and an exuberance which is very winning. He has also that rare quality of masculinity which is so valuable on the stage. There are excellent actors who, without being in any way effeminate, lack masculine appeal; and there are actors who are so in the grip of what Max Beerbohm called 'manlydom' that they are nuisances on the stage, for their manlydom expresses itself in all the most obvious ways—in noise, in overbearing mannerism, and in rumbustiousness; but the really masculine actor is the one who has masculine grace and gentleness and charm combined with virility, and Mr. Shatner is one of these lucky ones. He played Gratiano as a bore, with a ready and rattling laugh—but a young bore, to whom all may be forgiven for his gaiety; what such a man would be at forty we are not obliged to enquire. It was an excellent performance, which deepened suddenly and repellently in the Trial Scene. As this progressed Gratiano became more and more enraged until, as Shylock was about to leave the court, he spat full in his face. It was a shocking moment, but it was a moment of truth. For which of us has not had the experience of seeing a friend betray himself in some ugly passion, showing as in a lightning-flash a dark abyss in his nature at which we had not guessed? Here we saw that, like so many jolly good fellows, Gratiano could be a dangerous and brutal man.

HIGH COMEDY

NERISSA WAS PLAYED by Helen Burns in a style that admirably complemented that of Portia and Gratiano at once. Where her mistress was dashing and adventurous, she was reluctant and apprehensive; the exploits which Portia proposed with all the careless enthusiasm of a leader, she considered with the realistic eye of a follower who would undoubtedly be called upon to do much of the work. Where Gratiano was bold and winning, she was reserved and guarded. Her whole performance was a beautifully controlled and witty commentary on the extravagances of those around her. Miss Burns is especially gifted in the matter of her face, which mirrors her thoughts with fine subtlety; it is not that she pulls faces, or indulges in the 'double-takes' and eye-rollings of comedians of the baser sort; it is rather that she follows the action with an alert blankness of expression which imperceptibly changes to incredulity, or misgiving, or disappointment, or secret glee without any discernible movement of the features. Such a moment was her entrance in the Trial Scene, dressed as the lawyer's clerk; a less confident clerk was never seen, but her terror was given to us without tricks. This was a comic performance

BASSANIO

Sleeves removed
for Trial Scene
+ Cloa
Worn.

on a high level, and it added much to the quality of the whole.

BASSANIO, FAR MORE THAN LORENZO, demands high romance from the actor. The character does not bear logical examination; there is no point in probing Bassanio for psychological subtleties. What is required of the actor is to fill out the sketch which Shakespeare has given to the dimensions of the hero in a fairy-tale. Bassanio has some fine poetry to speak, and some telling situations in which to display himself. It is up to him to make the most of his opportunities. He needs a heroic presence, a fine voice, and the ability to suggest romance on the highest level.

Donald Harron is not an obvious choice for such a role as this, for he is primarily a comedian. There is about his personality a crisp and sparkling quality which is a very different thing from the warm effulgence of the romantic hero. He can submerge it in such a part as that of Octavius in *Julius Caesar*; the chilly calculation of that ambitious youth is well within his scope. He can give us a hero who is not entirely heroic—who has a dash of character—as he did when he played Bertram in *All's Well That Ends Well*. But Bassanio has no character other than that of Prince Charming; the actor must, so to speak, bring his character with him. That is what Mr. Harron did, and he gave us a Bassanio who was handsome, witty, and at the same time oddly boyish and gauche. These latter attributes were assumed; Mr. Harron need not be boyish or gauche unless he chooses. Apparently he assumed these qualities in order to make Bassanio likeable, because he could not play the part in the high heroic strain in which it is written.

It must be said at once that there are not many actors who could do so. That quality of high romance is out of fashion nowadays except in ballet, where we see it exemplified in the great *danseur noble*—Youskevitch, for example. We are assured by critics of an earlier era that several actors of the late Victorian and Edwardian period possessed it; those of us who have seen some of those actors after their youth had gone have recognized what they must have been at their best; the passing of time had sometimes marred romance with pomposity, but a glowing tenderness and splendour was still fitfully apparent. But this is not in Mr. Harron's line.

If he did not show us the full romantic quality of Bassanio he gave us much for which we were grateful. His ardour in describing Portia to his friend was moving, and his deep concern when he was to make his choice among the caskets was finely suggested. But when he turned to claim the waiting Portia he gave a giggle which was not that of a triumphant suitor in the noble mould. In all of Bassanio that was capable of being played as comedy he delighted us, but the moments of high romance eluded him.

PORTIA AT FULL LENGTH

PERHAPS THIS WOULD NOT HAVE BEEN a subject for comment if Portia had not been at her best in these very moments. Frances Hyland is an actress who appears to do everything by art and nothing by nature. This is not said in dispraise, but in an attempt to explain her style of acting; she is a splendid technician; she never struggles or seems possessed by an idea which she cannot communicate. She had determined on a Portia who was a very great lady, and she conveyed that idea with complete success. We wanted her to be won by a Bassanio who was a very great gentleman.

BASSANIO'S TRAIN

The brilliance of Miss Hyland's technique may be illustrated by an instance from the Trial Scene. She approached the Mercy Speech so gently that we were never troubled by that sense that a Gem from Shakespeare was coming, which even very good actresses cannot always avoid. She was well into the speech before we recognized it as something we had all memorized at school. And, at one point, she seemed to hesitate, to be unsure of what she should say next. A great many people were deceived into thinking that she had forgotten one of the best-known speeches in Shakespeare. But it was a telling effect, carefully conceived and successfully carried out.

Portia's conduct in the Trial Scene has been taken by many actresses as the foundation for her whole character. A woman who can argue down an opponent who has silenced the whole might of Venice must, they feel, be a woman of weighty intellect. And so they have played Portia somewhat heavily, as though all her wit and exuberance in the other scenes of the play were the relaxations of a female Blackstone. But it was not Dr. Guthrie's idea that Portia should come to court with her sleeves full of aces; she pretended to be assured, but she was

NERISSA

feeling her way until she found the solution to the case in a law-book, just in the nick of time. This was in keeping with the conception of the play as a fairy-tale. It also disposed of the difficulty which the other interpretation brings with it, which makes Portia seem to be playing cat-and-mouse with Shylock, admitting the justice of his case only to hurl him from a higher precipice at the end. This Portia appeared in court obviously hoping that Shylock could be bought off, and when he refused the money she was in a desperate predicament. When an appeal to mercy, and an offer of money, had failed, she fell back upon her mother-wit

PORTIA
IN THE TRIAL SCENE

and it served her well. This was consistent with the Portia whom we had seen mocking her unwanted suitors, and who had surrendered herself to Bassanio in a speech of great tenderness and nobility.

Many descriptions are to be found of performances of Portia by great actresses of the past which leave us full of admiration for them. But until recent times they did not give us Shakespeare's Portia in full, for they shrank from certain passages which, in the words of one eminent Victorian critic, 'virtue and taste must always wish to be excised from this otherwise supreme conception of pure

73

NERISSA
IN THE TRIAL SCENE

womanhood'. Nowadays we are not so convinced that pure womanhood may not relish a joke about sex; purity, we feel, is at least as much a matter of how a thing is said, as of what is said. The lines in which Portia and Nerissa reproach their husbands for the loss of their rings do not seem to us to be outside the range of ladies of high spirits, who know how to turn a phrase. Miss Hyland was able to give us this side of Portia with all the lightness it demands. *The Merchant of Venice* is, among many other attributes, a comedy of sex, and it is good to see all the wit of the Fifth Act restored and played for its full effect.

Let us not leave this performance without commenting on the grace of Miss Hyland's stage deportment. She moves like a dancer, and wears her costumes perfectly. We are fortunate indeed that we need not look outside Canada for an actress who can give such splendid life to one of Shakespeare's loveliest heroines.

A PASSIONATE SHYLOCK

SHYLOCK, MUCH MORE THAN PORTIA, has been the subject of extreme and often misplaced ingenuity. The actor-managers of the nineteenth and early twentieth century, determined to make *The Merchant of Venice* into a play in which they could star, with a leading lady, laid heavy emphasis on Shylock's misfortunes as a father; they squeezed remarkable pathos out of his single reference to Leah, who gave him the turquoise (and who is never, it must be pointed out, identified as his wife); his references to his Jewish faith were solemnly underlined. Sir Henry Irving built up the part by a device which is so striking that it won the approval of discerning critics in his day; after the elopement of Jessica with Lorenzo, when the masquers had dispersed and the stage was empty,

Shylock, with his staff and lantern, was seen to return to his home, crossing a bridge which spanned a canal; he knocked at his door, and as the curtain fell he was waiting for his daughter to open it. This is a fine imaginative stroke, and I for one would like to have seen it. Sir Herbert Beerbohm Tree, with his restless anxiety to go Irving one better, did the same thing but continued the action until Shylock had let himself in with his own latchkey, only to rush back upon the stage in an ecstasy of grief and rage. That was too much. Other actors cut out Salanio's description of Shylock's public rage, and introduced a scene in which the Jew stormed across the stage, pelted by jeering children. Of several Victorian actors it was said that they made this role typify the suffering of the whole Jewish race. To such excesses does the star system lead when it is applied to ensemble plays. For *The Merchant of Venice* is an ensemble play, and Shylock is one of four leading parts.

In many ways his part is the best and most memorable, but that is not the same thing as a part to which all others are subordinate. If the play is turned into a background for a personal creation it ceases to be the play that Shakespeare wrote.

Frederick Valk played Shylock as the character appears in the text. He did not attempt to make the Jew a type of all Jews; he was content to make him one man, and that the villain of the play. His conception was powerful rather than subtle. He did not attempt to surprise us with ingenious sidelights on Shylock; his aim was to astonish and appal us with a full-blooded depiction of a man driven to an extreme course of action by ill usage, and in this he succeeded fully. His performance mounted like a great wave from the first scene in which he appears until the end of the Trial Scene, where his passion reached its height, and broke upon the beach. It was an astounding exhibition of mounting emotion, possible only to an actor of great physical and vocal resource. This was acting of a kind which we have not seen before at Stratford—acting which is uncommon in the English-speaking world, though a style favoured in Europe—and it roused the first-night audience to give Mr. Valk a standing ovation, which he had clearly not expected.

There were those who said that this tribute was because Mr. Valk, himself a Jew, had appeared as a Jew of villainous temperament. I for one do not believe this to be true; comparatively few people are obsessed by this question of who is, and who is not, of the Jewish faith, and theatre audiences do not reserve their warmest approbation for shows of good sportsmanship. It was a tribute to a stirring piece of acting, as was the similar ovation given to Alec Guinness on the first night of *Richard III*.

One somewhat unexpected characteristic of this Shylock was his geniality in his first scene. He did not fawn; he faced Bassanio and Antonio firmly, and with a hint of ironic insolence. He suggested the bond with the forfeit of a pound of flesh not as a calculated scheme to murder his enemy, but as a spur-of-the-moment joke, obviously thinking it the most ridiculous thing in the world. His treatment of Launcelot Gobbo was impatient, but not harsh, and in his passages with Jessica he was fatherly, but not sentimentally so. This Shylock, in his early scenes, was a man as much at ease in his world as the restrictions laid upon his race would permit.

This early sense of well-being provided an excellent contrast with Shylock as he appeared when robbed of his daughter and his money. If we see a Shylock who is too subtle and nervous, his rancorous pursuit of revenge does not greatly surprise us; this man, who seemed so sure of himself, presented a shocking figure when he became obsessed with the desire to kill his enemy. Yet there was no raving, no sobbing—only a frightening force of purpose, when he confronted his Christian tormentors. The great speech which begins 'To bait fish withal', which has always been a high moment in any performance of this part, was given by Mr. Valk with quiet fury. It was in the scene which follows, with Tubal, that he gave way to violent emotion.

Sir Henry Irving referred to certain parts in the plays in his repertoire as 'table-legs', because upon their firm support rested an important section of his own performance. Tubal is a table-leg. Bruno Gerussi was suitably firm and helpful, but he was dressed in the only really bad costume in the production; no actor can rise above a rig-out that makes him look like a bearded lady who has allowed herself to run to fat. Beyond this handicap, a good performance was discernible. Tubal was phlegmatic, and gave Shylock his news, good and bad, with the same air of resignation. Shylock's exultation when he heard of Antonio's misfortune was close to madness, but in the next scene, when he met his enemy with the gaoler, he was utterly self-possessed, and icy in his refusal of mercy.

Shylock appeared in the Trial Scene plainly assured of his victory. He barely concealed his contempt for the proceedings, and his reply when the Duke suggested mercy to him was given in the tone of a sharp rebuke. It is unusual to see a Shylock as bold as this, but the concept fits well with the fairy-tale nature of the play; Shylock is the powerful evil magician before whom even the constituted powers of law are abashed. He was patronizing and almost jaunty in his attitude toward the young judge who came to settle the case, and frankly contemptuous of Gratiano. His certainty of success was so great that even when Portia uttered the judgement which reduced his hopes to ruin he did not at first comprehend it. He looked at her incredulously, and laughed the laugh that we had first heard when he proposed the bond to Antonio. Then, as the reality of his situation broke upon him he lost, but only for a moment, his self-possession, and quickly recovered it to meet his altered situation.

It is easy for Shylock to garner sympathy at the end of the Trial Scene by suggesting that he is suddenly stricken by mortal illness; Richard Mansfield used to thrust his knife under his gaberdine in such a way that Shylock seemed to have stabbed himself; he made his exit as though bleeding to death. There is no warrant for such extreme antics. Shylock is a villain, and he meets a villain's fate. But if he is true to his villainy we admire him as we admire any show of constancy, however wrong-headed. Mr. Valk did not play for our sympathy at the end by tricks; he showed us, instead, a man whose world has fallen into ruins. He hardly seemed to notice the Christians who exulted in so un-Christian a fashion all around him. It was his inner agony which possessed him; physical insult was an old story to him, but spiritual defeat was a new experience. And so we saw him leave the court, surrounded by a cruel mob, but by his own reckoning completely alone.

A HEART-WARMING PRODUCTION

THOUGH SOME OF THE WORDS of criticism in the foregoing may seem to suggest a pernickety dissatisfaction, they are intended only to record particular aspects of what was, considered as a whole, a noble and heart-warming production of a great comedy. It is the fashion in some critical circles at present to decry anything which may be labelled as 'escape'. Yet *The Merchant of Venice* is escape. It contains nothing of that realism which gives photographic detail of the accidents of daily life: it is, on the contrary, a fine example of that other realism which provides us with a poetic distillation of our deepest wishes and our richest emotional experience. Shakespeare was at home with both these varieties of realism, and knew the value of both, but he gave unquestioned precedence to the latter.

BY THE END of the Festival this enchanting production
had coarsened perceptibly, and called for re-rehearsal.
What had been speed had become mere haste, and
some of the high spirits had given place to rowdiness.
Very frequently in his productions Tyrone Guthrie
calls for the effect of high-bred people behaving rather
badly; if the high breeding is lacking, the bad behaviour
becomes objectionable. Some effective pieces of by-play
had been lost. For instance, at the end of the Trial
Scene, a priest who had seen Shylock abused and spat
upon burst into bitter tears; this was a reminder that
Christianity was not fully represented by Gratiano and
the other Venetian bully-boys; but this effective comment
on the action had dwindled to nothing. . . . It was unfortunate that in this play, as compared with the others,
the text had suffered from transpositions, dropped syl-
lables and dropped words, and even alterations. Actors,
in their innocence, are inveterate improvers on Shakespeare if they are not held in firm check. Indeed, the
Shakespearean texts as they have come down to us show
many signs of having been nibbled by actors. But this
is not an excuse for continuing a bad practice; we must
be faithful to the purest text we possess. A wrong word
in Shakespeare is as execrable as a wrong note in Mozart;
Toscanini does not tolerate wrong notes and Dr. Guthrie
and his assistants should not do so, either. There are
theatres in which every fault in the text is marked every
night by the prompter, and every actor is fined according
to his faults, the money going to an actors' charity. Such
a system would not be amiss at Stratford, if we seriously
hope for a great Shakespearean theatre there.

A NOTE ON STYLE IN ACTING

By ROBERTSON DAVIES

A SOLDIER'S TALE
by Igor Stravinsky and C. F. Ramuz

CAST

NARRATOR	William Needles
SOLDIER	Douglas Rain
DEVIL	Marcel Marceau
PRINCESS	Lillian Jarvis

ORCHESTRAL ENSEMBLE

VIOLIN	Alexander Schneider
CLARINET	Ezra Schabas
BASSOON	Nicholas Kilburn
TRUMPET	Ellis McLintock
TROMBONE	Ted Roderman
BASS	Gurney Titmarsh
PERCUSSION	Harry Nicholson

Translated from the French by LAURE RIÈSE

COSTUMES BY CLARENCE WILSON

DIRECTED BY DOUGLAS CAMPBELL

CONDUCTED BY PAUL SCHERMAN

DURING THE MUSICAL SEASON which was part of the Stratford Shakespearean Festival of 1955 widespread attention was drawn by several performances of *A Soldier's Tale,* by Stravinsky and Ramuz, in which the celebrated French mime, Marcel Marceau, played the role of the Devil. This remarkable artist cannot be neglected in any consideration of the dramatic part of the Festival, and his art, as shown at Stratford, provokes some reflection on the matter of style in acting.

Because *A Soldier's Tale* does not suffice for an evening's entertainment, the performance opened with a programme of solo mime by Marceau, and this was a very happy circumstance, as will subsequently be shown. He appeared in the close-fitting garments and the chalk-white face of the classical mime, and created for us illusions of a man walking against a high wind, a man climbing a circular staircase, and a man in a tug-of-war team. We were at once conscious that we were watching an artist of uncommon quality, for though most of us had seen displays of this sort done by mimes of various degrees of proficiency, very few of us had ever seen them done with so much grace, so much economy, and so much direct communication with the spectators. Mime is, of course, wordless communication; sometimes, when the actor is miming, let us say, the threading of a needle, it is done with so much deliberation, and such accuracy of imitation, that we are almost convinced that we see the needle and the thread. But Marceau dispensed with all elaboration, all detail, and gave us the essential *idea* of what he was doing. When he was engaged in the tug-of-war, he was not a particular man pitted against particular opponents; he was the essence of all men in all

83

tug-of-war contests; he was many men; he was a length of rope. Many years ago, in a forgotten film, the late John Barrymore gave an imitation of an Arab leading a reluctant camel; he was Arab and camel in one, inextricably but clearly. Marceau, with infinite grace, proceeds along these lines. He shows us not appearances, but essences.

Consequently he is able to break away from mere imitation, which soon grows wearisome, and show us something as complex and as beautiful as the creation which he calls 'Youth, Maturity, Old Age and Death'. In the beginning he stood motionless and passive, eyes closed, in a posture which we recognized as that of the child in the womb; he stirred, he struggled for life; he moved with the uncertain, stumbling steps of a child; the free, light movements of childhood gave place to the awkward stride of adolescence, and this in turn gave way to the eager walk of youth; maturity came, with full physical power and determination, to turn to a slower step, and then an effortful step, as the face lost its expression and the cheeks hollowed and the eyelids drooped; at last, after the painful hobbling of decrepit old age, the figure was still, sunk in upon itself in the last extremity of weariness; then, as a hand drooped limply, this remarkable cycle was complete. It was carried through in one unbroken pattern of movement, occupying perhaps three minutes, and it was impressive as only a fine artistic concept, brilliantly executed, can be. This creation alone is sufficient to establish Marceau as a master of his art.

He next gave us four incidents in the experience of Bip, a character of his own creation. Bip is one of those unfortunates for whom nothing goes right; taming lions, skating, travelling, or catching butterflies, Bip was always in trouble. It was extremely funny, and it was superbly done; the best thing about it was that it was not done too much. Bip had finished his antics and left the stage before we had time to grow tired of him.

For we do weary of these unfortunate creations of comic genius. Charlie Chaplin built his great reputation on a character very much like Bip. His Sad Little Tramp has won millions of hearts. Chaplin also knows that enough is enough. We can love the Sad Little Tramp for just so long, and if he is with us a moment longer he becomes an Ineffectual Little Nuisance. The humour of ineptitude is not inexhaustible. We are offended, at last, by the man for whom everything goes wrong; we sense that the root of his misfortune is in himself, and not in the world around him.

The third of Marceau's solo performances was called 'The Public Garden'. When it began he was a statue in the garden—one of those heroic, rhetorical French statues. Then, in rapid succession, he became the people one sees in such a garden—a good child, a bad child; an eager lover, a watchful girl; a nurse gossiping with a crony as she takes the baby for a walk; a father with too many children to care for; a priest reading his breviary—a host of people conveyed in essence but not in elaborate detail, and changing so rapidly that the garden seemed full of life until, suddenly, he was the statue again, and the illusion was over.

Having seen these wonders, we expected a great deal from *A Soldier's Tale*.

It would be unfair to say that we were disappointed, but it would be untrue to say that our expectations were fulfilled. But then—what had we expected? The music of *L'Histoire du Soldat* is familiar from concert performances and gramophone records. We knew that it was to be something unusual—a story told by a Narrator and a few actors, with a small orchestra on the stage. We

85

were prepared to be puzzled, but we hoped that we would be excited, as well. Our hopes were vague, and when the performance was over our slight sense of disappointment was vague, too. We could not put a finger on precisely what was wrong.

Everything seemed to promise an unusual and provocative experience. The production of the piece seemed adequate; the atmosphere of informality was quickly established. The orchestra played well, and the actors seemed, upon the whole, well suited to their roles. But something was wrong. Two guesses as to what it was may be attempted here.

First, *A Soldier's Tale* is a confused piece of work. Its story, of the Soldier who sells his violin to the Devil for a book of secrets, and at last marries a Princess, is not well-shaped. It is derived from a group of Russian fairy-tales, and while some fairy-tales are great creations, others are maundering and without dramatic point. The poet, Ramuz, has sought to give more poetic weight to his story than is inherent in it, by giving his Narrator frequent and repetitive bursts of rhetoric about the soldier's return from the wars. The Devil is similarly weighted with a significance which he does nothing to justify; indeed, most of the time he seems a very simple-minded fiend. We were moved to echo Miss Talullah Bankhead's famous judgement on a bad play: 'There is less in this than meets the eye.' Stravinsky's vital and interesting music cannot cover the fact that Ramuz has an inadequate dramatic sense.

Second, there was a confusion of styles of performance among the actors. William Needles was present on the stage as Narrator; he is a fine actor, but he was not required to act. He did, however, have occasion to use his fine voice, which contrasted oddly with that of Marceau who cannot speak, in a stage sense, at all. Like

86

Chaplin, he has a small, light, inadequate voice, which proceeded oddly from his splendidly expressive body. Douglas Rain, who played the Soldier, is an actor of great range and power and of the four players in this entertainment he was easily the best; but he was required to woo the Princess, who was Miss Lillian Jarvis, a dancer. As a dancer she is interesting, but she cannot act. And so we were confronted with the spectacle of four gifted people who were only rarely able to achieve real contact with one another. They were all doing their special things very well, but there was rarely any sense of unity. It is pointless to blame the director, Douglas Campbell, for this; the disunity is inherent in the work itself.

There were good moments, of course. Douglas Rain was admirable as the Soldier tempted by promises of wealth, trying to comprehend the mysteries of the stock market. When we were able to watch Miss Jarvis dance, without expecting her to convey anything except her own grace and technical skill, we were content. When Marceau was able to abandon speech, and treat us to a moment of diabolically anti-clerical mime, we were enchanted. It was pleasant to hear William Needles telling a story, when the story did not degenerate into empty repetition. But we had to take our pleasure as it came; we could never depend on it for five minutes at a time.

Nevertheless we may be grateful for the opportunity to see this work. If it was not fully a success, it was that extremely important thing, a seminal failure. The misjudgements of men of the stature of Ramuz and Stravinsky are quite likely to be more refreshing to the mind than the complete achievements of smaller men. The Stratford Festival will not be built on successes alone; there will have to be some failures, and if they are failures on a high level they may be extremely important for the artistic growth of the Festival and for the theatre in

Canada. *A Soldier's Tale* made us think about style in acting, for it was a confusion of styles. Is a style of acting that is characteristic of the Stratford Festival likely to emerge from it?

No one can answer that question. In the world of artistic creation there are no guarantees. Something like Habima might emerge from Stratford if the influences were right. Yet who would desire a Habima in Canada? We want a theatre with Habima's seriousness and artistry, but we want it to be characteristic of our own country. We are used to being told that we have no national character sufficiently determined to produce any unmistakably Canadian art. That may have been so even as late as 1945, but we appear to be developing a national personality very rapidly.

But before we can talk of a Canadian style, we must have some notion of what style itself means. Certainly it is not a bundle of mannerisms, or a tricky or eccentric way of acting and presenting plays. Style, if it means anything, emerges from within the artist, and in the theatre a few players and directors with style can infect those about them. Style is an attitude toward one's work, which must also involve an attitude toward oneself. Of style in living, Aldous Huxley has written: 'Every life is a work of art, and every spirit has its own distinguishing style, good or, more often, alas, indifferent or downright bad. Some people exist Miltonically and some Wilcoxically; some in the style of *Figaro*, others in that of *The Merry Widow*. The noble soul is born and bred to live the equivalent of a Piero della Francesca fresco or a statue by Donatello.' The actor brings his style with him to his role; sometimes the little artist rattles inside the big part like a pea in a bladder. Can Canadian actors develop a style of their own, something fine and supple, something more truly our own than an imitation of the London

88

or New York stage? That will depend on influences. What influences have been at work in Stratford?

The chief influence has been that of Tyrone Guthrie, under whose discipline it is possible for an actor to show any striking quality that he possesses. But there are qualities which Dr. Guthrie likes better than others; he likes acting of the dashing, boldly-stated kind better than quiet and allusive acting; he does not encourage actors to be lyrical and romantic in their approach to classical plays; he seeks great, sweeping effects rather than subtle illuminations of particular passages in the text. The success of his methods needs no proof, but he would be the last man to claim that they exhaust every possibility in the art of the theatre.

Strong influences, too, upon those actors who have been at Stratford for three seasons are Alec Guinness, Irene Worth, and Frances Hyland. These three have this in common: they have not been strikingly endowed by nature with fine voices and compelling presence, and they have acquired these attributes by hard work and thought. They have overcome handicaps, and their victory has put its special stamp on their art. They do not attack any role boldly, storming its great moments with irresistible force; their creations are made up of hundreds of carefully considered effects which, in the aggregate, give us something that is fine and memorable. They are not players in the heroic mould, who take the heavens of classic drama by storm; they reach the heavens, but by ladders which they have been at infinite pains to make, and then to conceal. Such players have been among the best in every great age of acting, and some of our Canadian actors will find their guides among them.

But not all, for we have had heaven-stormers at Stratford, too. Frederick Valk is one, and Douglas Campbell another. It is not to be supposed for an instant that these men have no technique; they are masters of technique. But they have the physical attributes which permit them to attack great roles head-on, and carry them through on the boldest and most daring lines. It is not necessary to elaborate the distinction. Nobody would think of casting Guinness as Oedipus; very few people would think of casting Campbell as Richard III. Either man might be cast as Shylock, but how very differently they would approach the part! Physical strength and size of voice must always be deciding factors in making an actor choose either the direct or the indirect approach to a great role. Both paths may lead to greatness.

If the Canadian actors could bring it about, they could supply a lack in the English-speaking world of today by evolving a splendidly lyric theatre, where the spoken word was supreme. The Stratford performances are, in the main, well-spoken, but it is possible to long for something far better than mere competence. There is no model, no mark to aim at. The New York stage is not distinguished for the splendour of its speech; the London theatre, though very much better, is rarely able to bring forward a production in which at least a few of the parts are not delivered in those strangulated and pinched tones which suggest the world of the tennis party rather than the world of poetry. The Canadians begin with a clean slate, for this is not a country where a special accent distinguishes the world of fashion and where many young actors would rather speak fashionably than speak well. This is, upon the whole, a country of flat and ugly speech; our actors already speak differently from the rest of their countrymen; they have nothing to lose and everything to gain by going much further, and learning to speak the best and most expressive English in the world. This is not madness; it could be done, though of course it would not be easy.

Stratford, in its third season, has won high praise. Mr. Brooks Atkinson, of the New York *Times*, saw the Old Vic company, the company at Stratford-on-Avon, and the Canadian Stratford within a few weeks; he placed the Canadian theatre between the other two in merit, the Old Vic being first. Stratford, then, is able to claim notice with the best work of this kind that the English-speaking world can show. It has some individuality, but not yet enough. It dare not be a follower for too many years; in some respect it must lead. Why should it not lead in thorough understanding, and beautiful delivery of Shakespeare's text? These actors are too good to become mere spouters—a company of elocutionists. But they are still far from a fine and individual standard of speech. Yet in this difficult realm, where no other group of actors, as a group, has attempted to excel, they might triumph greatly. Certainly the achievement of creating the finest lyric theatre in the English-speaking world would be worth the great effort it would cost. And such an effort would bring with it a fine and individual style.

MUSIC AT THE FESTIVAL

By BOYD NEEL

THE IDEA OF ADDING MUSIC to the season of plays at Stratford is not of recent origin. During the first Festival in 1953 a series of concerts was given in the theatre Tent. These concerts suffered somewhat from being the poor relation of the Festival. They had little publicity, and were swamped by the flood of glamour which, quite rightly, descended on the plays. The following year, there was again a suggestion of having music during the Festival, but everything was left until much too late, and nothing happened. It was, however, at the discussions which then took place that the seeds of the 1955 Music Festival were sown.

Fundamentally, the idea behind the programme of music was one of making the Festival more of a 'resting point' than it had been hitherto. Dr. Guthrie wanted to make Canadians more 'Festival minded', to persuade them to stay and browse around Stratford, absorbing the atmosphere, instead of rushing down to see a play and then rushing home again immediately afterwards. There would always, of course, be the 'special excursion' by train or bus which would cater to those whose work made it impossible for them to see the plays in any other way, but a Festival demands a more specialized type of audience if it is to fulfil itself completely. One of its major delights should be the discussion, at some neighbouring café, of the evening's performance, with a simultaneous speculation on the delights in store on subsequent evenings. This is impossible with the 'there and back' method of Festival going. It was thought that a first class Music Festival, running concurrently with the plays, might help to induce people to stay over and sample both. Whether this year's music had that effect, it is too early at present to ascertain, but the same faces were seen at many performances.

When it had been agreed to go in for music in a big way, the first thing to decide was what that way was to be. What kind of music? Where was it to be performed? When were the concerts to be held? How long were they to be? Should the artists be entirely Canadian? Many of these questions solved themselves automatically as plans developed, but in the initial stages there were endless discussions. Eventually it was decided to build the programmes around a series of concerts for small orchestra. It was thought that this would provide sufficient variety, while remaining within the limited budget possibilities. The first task, then, was to find a small orchestra capable of dealing with so large a programme in so short a time. We felt that only an organized body, trained as an ensemble and with some sort of established repertoire, would meet the case. There was no such group available. The solution, therefore, was to form a group and train it throughout the year, giving as many concerts as possible with it during that time. Having had some experience in organizing such bodies, I was asked to attempt it. Little did I know what I was letting myself in for.

By this time it was October 1954; we had nine months to bring our group to the required pitch. This should have been easily possible in normal circumstances, but we soon found formidable obstacles appearing in places we had never expected. We had first to choose a name for the group. The obvious one was the 'Stratford Festival Orchestra', and that was the original intention. It was pointed out, however, that the orchestra would play most of the year in other places, that there were other Stratford Festivals with which it might be confused, and that, if the musical side of the Festival was a failure, the name would not do much for the orchestra's future. After weeks of discussion, it was decided to revive a name once famous in Canadian music—a name with a great tradition. The story of the forming of the Hart House Orchestra will have to await telling on another occasion, since it would fill a moderate-sized book on its own account. It is sufficient here to say that it *was* formed despite obstacles both expected and unforeseen which were surmounted only by the selfless devotion of a few people who were keen enough to want it.

The orchestra played a few concerts during the winter season with success. To enable it to become an ensemble of international standing, it needed, of course, constant rehearsal. And here was the great problem which remains unsolved to the present day. Where were the necessary funds to come from which would enable the group to rehearse regularly? In March the position appeared hopeless. We had no funds and the orchestra, although in being, could not work. I tried every source I could think of to raise the necessary money. When all seemed lost, the Maclean Foundation came to the rescue with a magnificent gift which should have enabled the orchestra to rehearse at least twice a week through the spring. Alas, a subsequent and unforeseen increase in the rates of pay for the players made this generous sum inadequate. It looked like the knock-out blow for the Orchestra, the Music Festival, and the future. Hurried meetings were held, and it was decided to carry on with one rehearsal a week instead of two, and that the players would work as hard as they could at their parts whenever they could spare the time. Each member of the orchestra took his part home to study. Without the amazing loyalty and keenness of the players themselves, the Music Festival could never have taken place. Time and again when all seemed lost, and blow after blow fell, the players ex-

97

pressed their determination that this thing must go on. To them it meant much for the future of Canadian music.

We now had the basic ingredient of our musical scheme fixed, and the next thing was to decide how to garnish it. The plays had started in 1953 with the policy of ninety-eight per cent Canadian casts, the remaining two per cent being internationally known stars. This seemed to work. Many people probably came to Stratford, in the first place, to see actors like Guinness and Mason in the flesh, having known them well for many years on film. The plunge once taken, these slightly nervous visitors found themselves actually *enjoying* Shakespeare for his own sake and discovering that his plays, far from being schoolroom bores, were still, after 400 years, the most exciting theatrical entertainment ever devised by a human brain. We therefore worked roughly along the same lines with the music. Star artists were to be engaged for certain concerts, but the brunt of the work would fall on the finest home talent available. To direct this complicated business of bookings and programmes generally, it was necessary to have a Festival Director of Music. The choice was obvious. Louis Applebaum had looked after the incidental music for the plays since the Festival began in 1953, and it was chiefly his enthusiasm that brought the idea of a Music Festival to a definite shape. Lou started work with no office and no staff. Anyone who has had to arrange a series of concerts lasting for even one week will realize what he cheerfully took on. The ultimate success of the venture was due almost entirely to his work and enthusiasm.

Having decided to have a Music Festival of four weeks' duration while the plays were running, we had next to find somewhere to accommodate it. The Tent was unsuitable acoustically and, in any case, was being used for the plays. In Stratford there was a theatre which might do but there were many things against it. One day Lou arrived in Toronto in great excitement with the news that an edifice known locally as the 'Casino' might be possible. I immediately visualized chandeliers, red plush and champagne, and in my mind's ear I could hear the distant cry of the croupier. We tore down to Stratford at once, and asked for the Casino. There, in the park, right by the river and not five minutes' walk from the Tent we found a vast wooden building, not at all unattractive, which, from the outside, looked rather like a New England barn. On entering, when our eyes became accustomed to the gloom, we were confronted with a vast empty floor marked out into badminton courts. In one corner stood the decaying remains of a rostrum and shell from which strains of music (I do not know what kind) had evidently once emanated. There was not a chair, not a drape, not a sound of human movement; just a vast dusty emptiness. Lou clapped his hands. I expected a swarm of bats to descend from the dim vaults of the curved roof; instead, a thousand echoes greeted our ears. We looked at each other in despair. Even if we could make the place into the semblance of a concert hall, the acoustics would defeat us in the end.

Why it had ever been called the Casino I never discovered, unless the title was ironical. We felt there was, however, a certain 'something' about the place. For one thing, the location was ideal. It was not in the town, and yet was only a few minutes' walk from the main shopping centre. You walked out of the door on to the river bank, which meant a perfect promenade during intermission. Architects were consulted, and they pronounced the building capable of being converted.

There were problems, of course. The Concert Hall adjoined the lawns of the bowling club and part of it was used as a kind of club-house. Compromise and discussion eventually straightened that out. Then it was discovered that there would be only one washroom for an audience of a thousand people. What was to be done? Actually nothing was done, which, as one philosopher remarked, 'only goes to show'. I presume he was referring to the fact that it did not appear to matter what accommodation was lacking, such was the enthusiastic spirit in which the audiences came.

Eventually the fine old building was converted into a very reasonable Concert Hall seating just under a thousand people. This was not large enough, but it was the best that could be done at the time. Lou's idea was to make it as much 'in the round' as possible, with a view to future dramatic presentations. However, if you make a music auditorium too much in the round you are apt to get into trouble. It means, for example, that some unfortunate souls in the audience hear all the bass but no tune, while others hear only tune. And again one is faced with the eternal concert hall problem of which are the best (and therefore most expensive) seats. In the bad old days when concert-going was chiefly 'snob', the most expensive seats were naturally those from which you could be seen by the maximum number of people, even if you heard atrociously. These seats were obviously right in the front, and therefore nearest the orchestra, so that all you heard was the particular violin you happened to be sitting opposite, or the agonized grunting of the conductor, which can be very frightful in a long *crescendo*. Added to all this, you usually got a stiff neck from craning upward to try and see what was going on. Unfortunately this tradition lingers and the most expensive seats are still often the worst, even in this age where plus-fours are not unknown in the orchestral stalls at Covent Garden.

The Festival Concert Hall turned out to be far better acoustically than we had dared to hope, and with a little

100

subtly hung sacking, the 'myriad echoes' were successfully flouted. The platform in the round was splendidly effective for the production of Stravinsky's *Soldier's Tale* but not so effective for seating an orchestra. We found that in each place where we wanted floor space, there was an aching void. Another miscalculation in this stage was the size of platform. Our original idea had been to have only a small orchestra in our first season, and we designed accordingly. Later, we decided to have a choir at two concerts; we had not allowed for the extra space required, with consequent congestion on these nights. But such things are inevitable and expected in a first season, and the marvel was that there were not more of them.

The next decision concerned the type of programme to be performed. A Festival scheme can take two forms. There is, first, the Festival which celebrates a certain event or composer. You can have a Festival to mark the bi-centenary of composer X or one consisting entirely of the works of one man. A Festival of the latter type is usually held in a place which has been associated with the composer in question, such as Mozart and Salzburg, Wagner and Bayreuth, Leipzig and Bach. The Stratford plays are, of course, associated with the name of Shakespeare for obvious reasons. With the music, however, we had no peg of this kind to hang the programmes on. We could, I suppose, have had a Festival of Canadian music, but there is not, as yet, sufficient Canadian music of quality to fill a whole Festival bill. That we would have a certain amount of Canadian music was generally agreed.

We come then to the other form of Festival where any type or period of music is performed without any special theme or central idea running through it. All we knew was that we were fixed as to the size and kind of the forces to be employed. This fact at once directed the choice of music into certain channels. For instance, we knew that, having an orchestra of only twenty-five or so players, we could rule out performances of any of the larger symphonic works in the repertoire. The repertoire of the chamber orchestra is vast but not familiar to a public soaked in Beethoven and Tschaikowsky. Some method of attracting audiences had to be devised other than that of trading on the works of lesser known composers. The method we chose was names. This had been the plan used on the dramatic side, and it had worked. When we had decided on this, work commenced on the building of the programmes.

Anyone who has had experience of this kind of thing will tell you that the most complex jig-saw puzzle ever devised by man is child's play in comparison. You decide that you will have a violin concerto which will fit very well with certain other pieces in a programme. You think Signor X would be just the person to play this. Signor X would be delighted, but can only arrive one hour after the concert has finished, as he will have to fly from Los Angeles where he is playing the night before. You move the violin concerto to the following night to find that, as that concert will be broadcast, you cannot fit it into the available time. You try again. Could Signor X come two weeks later and arrive a day early for rehearsal? Yes, he could. All seems well until it is discovered that the orchestral material for the concerto is not available at the later date as it is on hire in another country. And so it goes on. Telegrams, 'phone calls, midnight conferences, early morning planes to New York, and so on. All this would tax a highly trained staff in a fully equipped office. When we realize that Lou Applebaum, practically single-handed, dealt with the arranging of the entire Festival in a most efficient way, we marvel at the achievement. That all went smoothly and according to plan is an everlasting feather in his cap.

The drawing up of the programmes proceeded, in the manner I have just described, all through the spring and early summer. Another complicating factor was that many of the concerts were to be broadcast. Without the splendid co-operation of the Canadian Broadcasting Corporation, it is doubtful whether there could have been a Music Festival, but it made the programme building a formidable, and sometimes apparently hopeless task. Suppose the C.B.C. planned to broadcast part of a concert starting at, say, 9.05 p.m. and ending at 10.30 p.m. The start of the whole concert was at 8.45 p.m. each night. This meant that we had to think of some piece about fourteen minutes in length with which to commence the concert. We then had to fit music exactly into the period 9.05-10.30 for the remainder of the evening, leaving certain intermission gaps at set points. It can be imagined how well-nigh impossible this was. I think I can truly say that none of the programmes would have been in the order in which they finally were given if we had built them as straightforward concerts. I have gone into this at some length as I doubt whether the average member of the audience, who may have had a grouse about the order of the programme, fully realized what we were up against.

The final set of programmes formed an interesting group. There was much music which was quite unfamiliar to the Canadian audiences, and there were many performers of international reputation who took part. One of the things which took as much discussion as anything was *when* to have the concerts. Would the music draw off the play-going public and vice versa? Should the concerts be morning, afternoon, early or late evening? The answer to the first question was established before the Festival had even finished; the concurrence of plays and music had *no* effect on the audience attendance at either house. On several occasions both Tent and Concert Hall were filled to overflowing on the same night.

Time of day also seemed to mean little; if the public wanted to hear anything very much, it came, whatever time it might be. As far as I know, no pattern of any kind has emerged and the musical public remains the enigma it has always been. Big names draw or fail to draw. Certain composers draw, others do not. Who, for instance, could possibly have forecast that Vivaldi would outrival Bach in popularity? Such a thing would have been regarded as fantastic a few years ago, but that was our experience. What does it all mean? For one thing, a great change is taking place in the public taste owing to the ubiquitous long-playing record. Composers who, until recently, were names in a text-book, have suddenly become vibrantly alive as the sound of their music has begun to fill thousands of homes. As the musical past becomes more and more the present, and the older composers begin to emerge in all their glory, a completely new panorama is revealed. Mr. Pleasants* can cry havoc to his heart's content. It ceases to worry the average music lover, who daily discovers that there is nothing new in the musical heaven or earth. Vivaldi, Frescobaldi, Torelli, Pergolesi, and all the rest are with us once again. For how long, I will not prophesy, knowing, as I do, how these things go in cycles, but at the moment we must take notice of it. The Stratford programmes were, of course, much influenced by this 'new look'. The Vivaldi concert turned out to be one of the outstanding events and, artistically, was certainly one of the most satisfactory. Three eminent Canadian violinists joined forces in the Concerto for Three Violins, and finished the concert (with Mr. Alexander Schneider) by giving a superb per-

*Henry Pleasants, author of *The Agony of Modern Music*, Simon and Schuster, 1953.

formance of the newly revived Concerto for Four Violins in B Flat. This masterpiece is, in my opinion, finer than the well-known work in B Minor, which was the only composition of its kind played to any great extent during past years. The fact that Bach had admired it sufficiently to re-set it for four pianos had always been its chief claim to fame. The B Flat work is a far greater and more mature composition, and I hope it will retain its place in the repertoire.

The opening concert was in the nature of a tribute to Saint Cecilia' and Benjamin Britten's 'Hymn' to the Festival Chorus, which made its début during the season under its talented conductor Elmer Iseler, Purcell's 'Ode to Saint Cecilia' and Benjamin Britten's 'Hymn' to the same saint were sung. The Festival commissioned Dr. Healey Willan, dean of Canadian composers, to write a short choral work called 'Song of Welcome', with words by Nathaniel Benson, to be performed on the opening night. The orchestra played Honneger's Symphony No. 2.

We thought that we had prepared, during the weeks of preparation, for any emergency. We were wrong. For some weeks before the Festival the weather had begun to get uncomfortably hot, but not unusually so for the time of year. On the day of the opening concert, a heat wave of unparalleled ferocity descended on Ontario. The mercury soared to heights greater than anything yet recorded in this region. And not only for a few days. For the whole four weeks of the Festival there was not one moment of merciful respite for performers or audience. I shall never forget that opening concert as long as I live. The temperature on the floor of the hall was 105° at the beginning of the evening. What it must have been on the platform by the end, I cannot imagine. The fingerboards of the string instruments were running with water, making accurate playing practically impossible. Members of the Choir were overcome and had to leave. I can remember little of what happened, but I do recollect seeing, every now and again, a vague mass of faces in front of me, until more perspiration ran into and over my eyes, blinding me yet once again. Surely no concerts can ever have been given under such adverse circumstances. But adverse conditions are often a challenge to people of spirit and I shall never cease to admire the way the singers and players fought and, to a great extent, conquered. We had agreed that the orchestra should, for the Festival, wear white tuxedos. After the opening night, we decided that our only choice was to play wearing as little clothing as possible, and for the rest of the season we abandoned everything save shirt and trousers. Later, fans were put on the platform, and this relieved our suffering to some extent. Jokingly, people remarked that on the last night of the Festival the weather would probably change. Sure enough, as the last note sounded at the final concert, heavy rain descended and a cool breeze swept through the hall. This was the crowning insult to add to our injury.

To revert to our programmes: music of every period was represented and we played as much Canadian music as would fit into our scheme. I have already mentioned the Willan choral work, especially written for the opening concert. Other Canadian works which caught the fancy of the audience were the Two Études by Godfrey Ridout, the Divertimento by Oskar Morawetz, which received its first performance anywhere, the Suite for Harp and Strings by Harry Somers, and John Weinzweig's 'Interlude in the Life of an Artist'. The brilliant harp playing of Marie Iosch in the Somers' Suite was one of the highlights of the concert. As soon as she touched the harp a string broke. The consequent delay and fuss of repair would have quite unnerved most artists, but she remained calm through it all and went on to an ovation at the close.

Other Canadian artists who had outstanding successes were Lois Marshall in Bach's 'Jauchzet Gott', Glenn

106

Gould in Beethoven's Second Piano Concerto and the Goldberg Variations of Bach, the three violinists, Albert Pratz, Noel Brunet and Eugene Kash in the Vivaldi concert, and the singers Elizabeth Benson Guy and Jon Vickers in Handel's 'Acis and Galatea'.

The performances of Stravinsky's *Soldier's Tale* were outstanding. Brilliantly played by a small group under the Canadian conductor, Paul Scherman, and produced in a most interesting and original way by Douglas Campbell, the famous piece made a profound impression as performed on the Concert Hall stage. This event was especially important from the fact that the superb and unique French mime, Marcel Marceau, took the part of the Devil. William Needles made an outstanding Narrator with a glorious resonant delivery. The first part of the evening was taken up with Marceau's own solo recital, which has made him world famous. I wondered whether the platform in the round would worry him at all, as I had always seen him hitherto on a proscenium stage, but he was able to adapt himself to the conditions without any difficulty.

A work which caused a great deal of interest was the Concerto for Two Violins by Mozart which Isaac Stern and Alexander Schneider played on July 13th. This splendid piece had not been heard in Canada before. Works which had, hitherto, been unfamiliar, but which the audience took to its heart, were the Symphonie Spirituelle of Hamerik, the Fugal Concerto of Holst (with two magnificent soloists in Perry Bauman and Gordon Day), the Triple Concerto of Vincent d'Indy, the Symphony for Strings by Jean Françaix, and Arthur Benjamin's Ballade for String Orchestra.

Among visiting singers were Aksel Schiøtz and Elisabeth Schwarzkopf, both of whom gave memorable *lieder* recitals. Miss Schwarzkopf also sang Mozart's 'Esultate Jubilate' and a Bach Cantata with the orchestra. The latter performance, with Perry Bauman and Rowland Pack playing the *obligati* superbly, was a most memorable one.

At the concert of July 27th the Festival Choir showed what a first class ensemble it had become under Elmer Iseler, when it gave a fine display of exquisite music movingly sung. The Choir was joined at this concert by Suzanne Bloch, daughter of the well-known composer, who played on various old instruments, giving a commentary on the music performed.

At the final concert it was decided to combine all the forces once more, and Handel's 'Acis and Galatea' was given in the original version without the usual Mozartian trimmings. The four young Canadian soloists gave a fine account of the lovely songs and the Choir sang the cheerful choruses with obvious relish. 'Acis and Galatea', like *Hamlet*, is 'full of quotations' and should have more frequent performances than it gets.

At the time of writing the future of the Musical Festival is undecided. There can be no disputing the fact that the Festival justified itself and that, in spite of the appalling heat, the performances were of a consistently high standard. There are, of course, many improvements which will have to be made in any future season. The Hall will need much done to it, not the least being the installation of some sort of ventilating system. There are many ways in which the musical horizon can be extended and much depends on the actual structural facilities available. The two things are quite interdependent. If you have a certain type of auditorium, it demands a corresponding type of work performed in it. It is a 'hen and egg' problem. Which is to come first? In the case of the plays, the theatre in the round more or less dictated the type of production and also the repertoire available. In the case of the music, the two struggled along together, neither quite knowing how the other was going to turn out. After the experience of the first season, a definite direction can now be taken for the future.

Personally, I should like eventually to see a great Festival of All the Arts established at Stratford. The town is ideally suited to such a gathering and with the growth of the artistic side there should come a greater awareness of the inhabitants themselves. This year there were already signs that Festival visitors were being considered in certain special ways. The crying need at present is for somewhere to gather after the performances. On the European continent, one of the greatest pleasures of festival-going is getting together after the show and the resulting discussion of the evening's events. At present, Stratford is rather woefully lacking in this respect; but even a great Festival like Edinburgh has never faced up to this problem properly, and the lack of restaurants and cafés which are open late in the Scottish capital during the Festival has always been one of the crying disgraces of that great gathering and has taken much of the pleasure from a visit there. As Ontario is for the most part blessed with beautiful summer weather, I should like to see many more outdoor cafés and restaurants in the Festival town. Outdoor events will eventually figure large in the Festival programme. Stratford is just the place for such happenings; and I doubt that the river and the island will remain merely a setting for the swans. Surely there must soon come a time when the island will be under Prospero's benign rule, and the wood moved to the outskirts of Athens.

There are so many ways of expanding. Opera and ballet are one's first thoughts, and I cannot see that inviting orchestra shell which stands in the park being long without the world's most beautiful open air music— the Serenades and Divertimenti of the eighteenth century. Also, a great Festival invariably generates a demand for a first class school to be held in conjunction with it.

The drama side already has its school well established, and this year a start was made on the musical side.

The Royal Conservatory of Music of Toronto took advantage of the presence of the famous soprano, Elisabeth Schwarzkopf, and extended its Summer School activities to Stratford where a master class in *lieder* was held. This proved to be an unqualified success, about thirty students availing themselves of the wonderful opportunity. The classes were held in the Concert Hall, and went on far beyond the official hours, so enthusiastic were both teacher and pupils. Miss Schwarzkopf gave unstintingly of her energy and sang a great deal during the classes, which were something the students will never forget. The superb pianist, Paul Ulanowsky, who accompanied Miss Schwarzkopf in her recitals, gave a course in the art of accompaniment for the Royal Conservatory students, which proved to be another outstanding event.

There was no doubt that this programme filled a need and a natural expansion of the idea will, I hope, follow each year. There is a great advantage in holding a school under these conditions. Students, as well as being taught by the world's finest artists, can take the opportunity of watching them work at first hand. Eventually student bodies can be incorporated into performances of large scale works, as is done in the drama department. Classes in all branches of musical study can eventually be held in closest co-operation with such a Festival, to everybody's benefit.

Stratford is capable of anything, and there is no reason why, in a few years' time, it should not become as famous as any of the great European Festivals. It possesses a Directing Board of enormous discernment and enthusiasm which is surely unique of its kind, and its policy is a wonderfully enlightened one.

THE PRODUCTION OF
KING OEDIPUS

by TYRONE GUTHRIE
and TANYA MOISEIWITSCH

THE PROCESS of preparation which precedes the production of a play varies very considerably with the nature of the play, and with the conditions—time, place, budget and so on—which govern the production. In this essay, then, rather than attempt any generalized description, we have concentrated on the preparation of one particular production which had interested us very much: the *Oedipus* of Sophocles. Much has already been written about this play. Historians, literary and dramatic critics, moralists, psychologists and poets have for centuries discussed it from their different points of view; they will continue to do so for centuries more. As is so often the case where dramatic literature is concerned, little or nothing has been written about methods of realizing the work in performance.

Without wishing in any way to belittle the contributions of learned men, one regrets that from the vast mass of scholarly criticism of dramatic literature it is not possible to get a clearer idea of what performances of *Oedipus* have been like. Who would not gladly trade many millions of words of grammarians' wrangling for a detailed, technical account of, say, the original production of even such comparatively recent works as *The Beggar's Opera* or *She Stoops to Conquer*? How much it would tell us not only about theatrical practice and outlook at the time, about changing public taste, but about the works themselves. And how much more valuable still would such information be about works of more remote date where even less is known about the public and theatrical context of their production. Quite apart from the technical interest of such accounts, they would illuminate a point which often eludes grammarians, that is the extraordinary influence of fashion upon the interpretation of a classic. In the light of contemporary attitudes to social and moral issues, a play can have a number of entirely different *meanings*; and works which seem lively and interesting in one period are bores in another.

The practitioner's approach is sometimes, but not always, unintelligent, often slapdash, often over-influenced by a desire to please audiences, which are more susceptible to shock tactics than to finesse. And though the practitioner is not immune from exhibitionism, yet neither is the scholar. Also we cannot help feeling that the practitioner's point of view is apt to be more lively than the scholar's because his theories must be submitted to the test of practice. They may not on that account be valid, but they are likely to avoid the worst excesses of pedantic niggling and learned silliness.

The following discussion of *Oedipus* must not, therefore, be regarded as anything other than the groping and fumbling approach of two collaborators who make no claim to scholarship, but only to some considerable practical experience in the theatre, and to a right to interpret this masterpiece according to their own limited but enthusiastic lights.

THE FACTS OF THE PLAY

To UNDERSTAND ANY PLAY it is necessary to make clear to the audience the facts which it relates. Drama is story-telling first and last, story-telling in its most direct form. The characters of a drama are impersonated by people who recapitulate the story in words and in action.

With any story of serious intentions, however, the mere facts—what happens next—are not important. The point is the style or manner in which it is told, and the comment which it attempts to make upon life and mankind in general. The story of the Prodigal Son, for instance, is not important so much because of what happens, but because very briefly, very memorably, very poignantly, it makes a number of shrewd comments upon the relation of all fathers to all sons, including that of a Heavenly Father to Prodigal Humanity.

An author need not necessarily be aware of the comment he is making. In fact, the most important and interesting comments frequently emerge without the author's conscious awareness, sometimes even in spite of his conscious intention to the contrary. Moreover, the same work may be very differently interpreted by different people and at different times, and such difference does not necessarily imply that one comment is more valid than another. Broadly speaking, the greatest works of art are susceptible to the greatest variety of interpretation; they do not fully reveal themselves to any one person at any one time.

Sophocles wrote *King Oedipus* about 254 B.C. It was entered for the great dramatic contest which was the centrepiece of the Spring Festival in which Athens honoured the god, Dionysus. Note that Dionysus is not, however, an important deity in the play which is dominated by Apollo. This may be because neither Sophocles nor most of his very sophisticated audience any longer believed literally in the existence of a heavenly family in which all the gods were 'children' of Zeus and Hera who dwelt literally on Mount Olympus and whose family life was a tumult of human passion uninhibited by the physical limitations of human beings. It is not unreasonable to suppose that Sophocles may have felt about the Olympians very much as a thoughtful man of our own day feels about the ferocious deity who dominates the Book of Judges: a conception of godhead which we believe to be a primitive one, which subsequent and more sophisticated societies have softened and rendered more subtle, have made to conform more closely to their own ideals. For it can hardly be denied that though we profess to believe that God created us in his image, none the less we create Him for ourselves in ours.

The aspect of Deity with which Sophocles is concerned in this play is Apollo, the God of Light, and thence, metaphorically, the God of Knowledge, of Revelation, of Intuition and Inspiration; the Sun God and therefore the source not merely of light but also of heat, of fertility—in short, a conception very little removed from any reasonable person's embodiment of Omnipotence and Immanence, a conception which is no less, and no more, acceptable now than it must have been 2,000 years ago.

Now it is necessary to recall briefly how the Athenian Festival of Dionysus came into being. In all epochs and in all climates the return of spring after winter has been, for obvious reasons, an occasion of thankfulness and joy. In very primitive society man expressed his emotion spontaneously and instinctively. Gradually his spontaneous reaction to the unexpected return of warmth and fertility was replaced by an annually recurrent, remembered and looked-forward-to joy, tempered by thankfulness to the Origin of the miracle. This recurrent and more sophisticated reaction resulted in recurrent and more sophisticated expressions and emotion. Moreover, the recurrent season of fertility induced primitive man not only to feel but to act. There were seeds to sow in the earth. Man, the sun's image, feeling the joy and vigour of spring in his body, nourished again after a winter of short commons, must plant his own seed in the body of Woman, the image of the Earth. Rain must be prayed for, begged, induced to fall and fertilize the earth. It is not hard to guess the very broad outlines of primitive rites of spring. These rites in Athens were focussed on

Dionysus, an impersonation of joyous intoxication, of many ideas and emotions associated with fertility, liberation from bondage, the relations of male with female.

For the purpose of this essay we need not discuss in detail the Dionysiac rites, except to say that generations before Sophocles they included the sacrifice of a beast, itself almost certainly a symbolical substitute for the human sacrifice of still earlier times. The story of Abraham and Isaac is an interesting parable of precisely such a process. In the story as related in Genesis the beast is miraculously substituted for the human. As so often, a miracle accounts *tout à coup* for an individual change of heart which normally occurs collectively over a span of many generations, a slow process of social and moral evolution.

Gradually, as Athens became richer and softer and gentler, public opinion was repelled by the public slaughter even of a lamb or a kid; and, by a still further process of substitution, the sacrifice was now merely enacted ritually by priests in narrative and mime. One cannot but be reminded of the Christian rite of Holy Communion, where the human sacrifice of Christ—the breaking of the body and the spilling of the blood of the Lamb of God—is re-enacted by a priest in narrative and by the symbolical breaking of bread and pouring of wine. Even in the time of Sophocles sacrifice was already expressed by narrative and mime which was no longer literally concerned with ritual slaughter. Tragedy was considered to pay sufficient tribute to the god by recapitulating half-secular legends on the *theme* of sacrifice, now refined to mean expiation by means of suffering.

Just as the participants at Holy Communion commemorate Christ's sacrifice, so, presumably, the Athenian audience at the Dionysiac Festival partook of the Passion there commemorated. Reverent spectators of the Passion

117

of *Oedipus* will surely have felt their own 'communion'
with his agony.

AT AN EARLY STAGE of preparation it was necessary to
decide which translation of the play should be used. The
choice was bewildering, but fairly soon two main alter-
natives emerged. Some translators were primarily concerned with being faithful to the original text of Sophocles, and only secondarily interested in the effect of
their own version. Others were prepared to sacrifice exact
correspondence with the author's literal meaning in order
to make his general intention more acceptable.

We plumped for the second school of thought. The
literal translations were, most of them, barely readable;
and when spoken aloud the effect was positively absurd
—clumsy, unrhythmic, unmelodious sentences that bore
no relation to human utterance.

So many scholars have supposed that the meaning of
a play can be abstracted from its form that, in this play
for instance, the speeches can be rendered in a form
which is not only utterly unmusical but, in its laudable
desire to be faithful, almost unintelligible. This arises
because many scholars never think, even reject with re-
pugnance, the idea that a play has been written to be
acted, that its lines are the score of a symphony. To many
scholars great plays are 'texts' first and last, to be absorbed
by the intelligence alone and unassisted by the senses,
except for the use of eyes to interpret the letters of the
printed page. Again and again instances arise of Shakespearean scholars who because of their blindness and
deafness to theatrical effect, and because of their childlike ignorance of how and why theatrical effects are produced, miss implications, labour the obvious and, in short,

make asses of themselves. Scholars, with no less justification, level exactly analogous charges at those who think theatrical skill and experience suffices without scholarship. The one point of view is as foolishly narrow as the other.

Of the English translations which have some pretension as dramatic literature, by far the best known are those of Gilbert Murray. His version of *Oedipus* is melodious, swings along on rhythms that are easy on the ear; his introduction to his version gives a considerable clue to the translator's intentions and personality and is a little masterpiece of its kind, a rare combination of modesty with learning, of learning with philosophy and philosophy with common sense. It may well be that Murray's translations will become the classic English versions of Euripides and even of Sophocles. But for us now his flowing and 'beautiful' translation conjures up only euphoric and scented Mediterranean visions of Leighton or Albert Moore. In this landscape one could only see plump, pretty, pink Englishwomen in 'Greek' fancy-dress in mauves and pinks and palest yellow, and undergraduates who, momentarily laying aside their cricket-bats, were making believe, in very upper class accents, to be Old Men of Thebes. The Murray version, in short, seemed to us to have sacrificed, in favour of a rather ninety-ish 'beauty', too much of the impersonal and removed grandeur of the original. While this may well be unimportant, it seemed to us dated. This may mean no more than that its particular kind of poetry and particular kind of drama are very temporarily out of fashion, and will come in again quite soon. It is not necessarily a condemnation of a work of art because from time to time it goes out of vogue. But if in the theatre one prepares a production of a work which *feels* out of date, there is every danger that the production will be dowdy and dreary. Respect and reverence alone do not generate the energy which is required to put a difficult play upon the stage. There must be enthusiasm. If enthusiasm is not there, then the task is better not attempted.

Of translations into English more modern than Murray's, the best seemed to us that of Watling, published in the late 'thirties, and an earlier one made for production in Dublin by the great Irish poet, William Butler Yeats. Of these two Watling's had the advantage of being far closer to Sophocles, far closer both literally and in intention. Yeats has made no attempt to 'translate'; he has retained the main structure of the original but has omitted whole passages whose meaning seemed to him to have become obscured by distance. He has made no attempt to reproduce the literary or dramatic style of Sophocles. He has missed much that Watling and other translators have attempted and often achieved. But of all the very many translations which we read, only that of Yeats succeeded in rendering the choruses so that the English versions were poems in their own right.

The Yeats choruses, though often quite far removed from the original, have a logic which reinforces the music and a music which reinforces the logic; the poems provide the necessary logical and musical bridge from one dramatic episode to another. We could imagine that in Yeats' version the Chorus could make a contribution to the performance which would be dynamic and not either just sentimental or else a difficult and interruptious bore.

Except for the choruses, the Yeats version is in prose; prose of a stern simplicity; prose of military terseness and practicality. The poet has been at pains to exclude anything that might seem to be added ornament or colour or artifice. There are hardly any similes, a minimum of descriptive adjectives; no high-falutin' poetical words are used; all the familiar clichés and dodges of rhetoric are eschewed. This makes of it a very aristocratic, but

austere and uncompromising document; it treads bare-
foot over steep sharp rocks. Compared to it, Murray's
is a rum-ti-tum-tumpty of purpurate passage through
meadows of asphodel azured with amaranth, down to a
sea that is silver in starlight.

Yeats had made the instrument that seemed to us to
fit the job. This gaunt prose suited the huge, abstracted,
slightly grotesque figures which we were beginning to
imagine; by being unadorned it was the more intelligible;
because the expression was brief and simple, it was not
less but more moving. Above all, in this version it was
possible to imagine the events of the play almost completely divorced from detail of time and place.

THE UNIVERSAL QUALITY

THIS ABSTRACT QUALITY was exactly what we wanted. We
were anxious to suggest that King Oedipus was not merely
the King of Thebes, the head and father of his people,
but was the image of the sacrificed beast, and thence an
image of human sacrifice: the one man whose death was
expedient for the people. It seemed to us highly significant that the 'death' of Oedipus was not literal extinc-
tion but that he was reserved for a mysterious and incredible end, like Enoch, or for that matter like Jesus Christ,
whose Passion was succeeded by a mysterious Resurrec-
tion, and that in turn by a no less mysterious Ascension.
Moreover, it seemed to us highly significant that the
Passion of Oedipus was expressed by self-blinding, by
cutting himself off from the light. In this play the close
analogy between light and God is inescapable. By destroying his own faculty of sight, by putting out the light of
the eye, he was destroying the light within himself. And
since, metaphorically, he was abhorring and rejecting his
own insight, the recognition of his own identity, he was,

both literally and metaphorically, destroying, or trying to destroy, a part of the god Apollo immanent in himself.

Again the analogy with Christian theology struck us. The victim had God within himself; this was not merely the Passion of a man, and an emblem of mankind, but also the Passion of a god. It seemed to be the expiation by God of a crime committed by his creature man, in whom was godhead immanent. What crime? What original sin?

We shall go back to this question at the end of this essay. Meantime let us pause and consider some of the results of our conclusions so far, in the practical terms of theatrical production.

This was not to be a story about a king called Oedipus, who ruled over a city called Thebes in an identifiable locality at some vague but still identifiable date. Oedipus was to represent a far more general conception, something that was concerned with manhood in general, King Humanity.

There must, therefore, be no *literal* suggestion, in the picture which we would set before the audience, of locality or date. Since the names of people and places were Greek, and since the script is full of suggestions that the tale is to be regarded as one of great antiquity, going back into the very roots of time and the springtime of the world, we decided that the clothes should suggest, but not literally copy, the heavy folds and severe lines of early Greek sculpture. For a time we considered the notion of a colour scheme in tender juicy greens and yellows which would literally suggest the springtime of the world, the Return of Dionysus, which would be in ironical contrast to the plague-stricken city, the doomed and ominous atmosphere which hangs over the whole play.

On second or maybe third, fourth, or fifth thoughts, this idea was rejected. It would result in a trivial look, we thought, too pretty and sophisticated; the play would look vogueish; the irony would misfire. We would plump for a sombre scheme but not, we hoped, one which would lose all suggestion of radiance. This was after all a play not only about darkness, but equally about light. Oedipus, Jocasta, and Creon must be royal. The Chorus must be ordinary, humble in the face of royalty. Their humility must itself exalt the mightiness of the great ones; their behaviour must suggest the critical servility of man to God; the critical servility of dogs to men.

Tiresias? The Messenger? They must wait. The main scheme must be determined. The main framework once decided, they could be fitted in.

THE CENTRAL FIGURE

OUR MINDS RETURNED TO THE CENTRAL FIGURE. Oedipus must suggest a king, a man, all men and yet no single man. He must also suggest his affinity with God—the particular aspect of godhead with which this play concerns itself—the God of light, the Sun. The Sun! He must be gold; wear a gold dress, a great gold crown with spiky rays, a sceptre of gold, a golden face.

Suddenly we apprehended that the only way we could get the feeling of universality, as opposed to particularity, of all men and yet no man was by hiding the faces of the actors, suppressing their own individual traits, obliterating their small particularities behind the impersonal, but not inexpressive, features of a mask. Suddenly we realized that this was one reason, if not the dominant one, why the Greek actors were masked—to obliterate particularity. Negatively, the actors must *not* suggest particularity; no detail of personality must intervene between the audience and the tragic symbol. Positively,

123

they must preserve the anonymity, the aloofness, of a priest celebrating mass. So far as possible they must be mere channels through whom the effluence of something greater than ordinary human stature might pass. And then we asked ourselves whether the use of the cothurnus to make them of greater than human stature was not equally indispensable. The great ones must be literally greater than their fellows.

We resolved, then, to experiment with high shoes, and with masks. About the former we had few serious doubts. There could be no insuperable practical difficulty, since the action of the tragedy never demanded any rapid movement. The masks were a more debatable problem. Could actors speak audibly from behind a mask? Would the immobility of the mask, after its first impact, become a bore?

Doubt was reinforced by the fact that the role of Oedipus was being played by James Mason. It seemed perverse to engage one of the handsomest actors of the day and then hide him behind a mask. It also seemed unreasonable to proceed any further without letting him know what we were planning. To succeed, the experiment would require the enthusiastic co-operation not only of those who were to make the masks, but also of those who were to wear them.

We wrote to Mason, told him the reasons for wanting masks, expressed our doubts, made it clear that we should not push him into a mask against his will but that we rather hoped he would be interested in the experiment. He replied at once, with characteristic modesty, that he would feel more confidence, not less, if he could attempt this extremely exacting role in the heaviest possible disguise.

We decided to go ahead. We agreed that it would be practical, by thickening the soles of their shoes, to raise the actors four to six inches higher than their natural height. The masks should be even larger in relation to the size of the natural face. We resolved to experiment with masks one-and-a-half times life size. This would, we realized, make Oedipus, Creon and Jocasta appear to be creatures with disproportionately large heads. The distortion was deliberate. The large heads, we believed, would create the desired effect of rather strange great-ness and impressiveness, would be another means of achieving the same aim as the judge's wig, the bishop's mitre, the guardsman's bearskin, the monarch's crown. In almost all ceremonial costume there is an attempt to enlarge and dignify the wearer by means of a sizable and heavily emphasized head-piece. Paradoxically, it is also the case that dignity is enhanced, not lost, when the head-piece verges on the grotesque, the inappropriate, the absurd. What, for example, could be more wildly un-suitable as a hat for a young girl than the British Imperial Crown? Yet it was precisely this unsuitability which enormously added to the poignancy, the dignity, the sig-nificance of the central moment of the coronation cere-mony of Queen Elizabeth the Second.

Since Oedipus was to come as a golden sun, it seemed to us logical that Jocasta should be a silver figure related to the moon. Creon, just less than of royal stature, later to turn tyrant, should be of baser metal—a head and robes of dark bronze.

Now, after two productions, we feel that, whatever the result may have been, the *plan* for Oedipus and Creon was a sound one. About Jocasta we have had second thoughts. She should not have been a silver figure related to the moon, quite apart from how this particular silver mask was designed and made. That idea is too cold, too chaste and too metallic. She should have been an earth-figure—warm in colouring, soft in contour: Mother Earth, the bride of the fertilizing Sun.

As it was, our original conception was that the great personages should look metallic in contrast to the Chorus who should wear life-size masks of a texture which should suggest wood or carved nuts, in dresses whose subdued low tones and soft folds should suggest, though not in at all a literal way, wooden figures corroded by moss and lichen, battered and twisted by winds and rain and frost.

So much for the general idea of the visual impression. The same consideration about the play would also govern its musical interpretation: absence of particularity, a removed grandeur. Obviously something was called for larger and simpler than the life-size speech of ordinary conversation. The almost chanted declamation of French tragedy seemed in some ways appropriate. But it did not agree too happily with the austere simplicity of Yeats and, with its boldly sustained vowels and powerfully accented consonants, it seemed too overwhelming for the intimate conditions of our theatre. Declamation which is impressive when spouted over footlights across an orchestra pit into a great Opera House would, even if brilliantly achieved, only be embarrassing in an auditorium where the remotest spectator sits only sixteen rows back and where the nearest sit, literally, at the actors' feet. And could it be brilliantly achieved? A style so sophisticatedly classical did not seem to exploit the virtues nor conceal the shortcomings of our company.

It was decided that we would try to evolve our own style in rehearsal. Obviously it must be more operatic and less natural than would be appropriate for Shakespeare; less so than the French style. We had at command some splendid voices, a highly intelligent, serious and flexible group of actors, a corporate spirit out of which something interesting might evolve.

126

It is not for us to say whether the eventual style of speech was successful or no. But we think it was reasonably consistent to a single convention, and that the Chorus had extraordinary discipline without all individuality being ironed out of the performers, and extraordinary vigour without being coarse. This was achieved only by many hours of rehearsal in the most favourable conditions, most of the time on the stage, much of the time in costume, in an atmosphere freed from a great deal of the strain and anxiety and haste attendant upon production for the commercial theatre; the kind of conditions which are all too rarely encountered, and which are only made possible by such an organization as the Stratford Festival.

THE MAKING OF THE MASKS

IN ORDER THAT THE SPEAKING should not be impeded, the masks would cover only the upper part of their wearers' faces. Beards on the actors' chins and jaws would meet matching beards and hair on the masks. The modelling of the faces was kept extremely simple. These were not to be realistic, but heavily stylized faces. Realistic masks, we considered, would not avoid the particularity of real faces. What we envisaged were masks which were no more than symbols of faces.

At one time we had the notion of making Picasso-like faces—two eyes on one side of a great triangular nose, and that sort of thing. This we discarded as being obtrusive, claiming attention and interpretation on its own account.

We settled for faces whose contours and expressions were very simple and easily apprehensible. The mask for Oedipus, for instance, was intended to be the simplest possible statement of intelligence and nobility in a context of suffering.

The Chorus masks, being life-size, enabled the actors to look through the eyes of the mask. In the great masks the eye holes were far above the actors' own eyes. Gauzed apertures in the cheeks of the masks made peepholes for their wearers.

Since we considered it impossible to put 'real' hair on faces which looked like metal or wood, the wigs and beards were made of tow, string, or felt, curled and twisted to look gnarled, severe or majestic as the expression of the mask demanded. Before the sketches were made, Jacqueline Cundall, the head of the Property Department at Stratford, was called in at the earliest stage of planning, and various materials were discussed. We had primarily to consider the comfort of the actors who would be wearing the masks in a tent at the height of summer under tremendously hot lamps. The masks must not only be light in weight but durable, to withstand sweat pouring down the actors' faces. It was finally decided to make them of chamois leather. Jacqueline Cundall had considerable experience in mask-making, and studied every angle of the sketches, keeping closely in touch with us over the important questions of proportion and expression. The designs for the masks grew from rough sketches which had been made in Rome of terracotta figures in the Villa Giulia, early Etruscan in date. These sketches were developed into working drawings of un-naturalistic but individual expressions of the characters as the ideas for the production became clear. Specifically, Creon has, on his first entrance, to signify that he is the bearer of good news by wearing a crown of laurel. This motif was used to represent not only a crown but the hair and beard of the figure, and the laurel was not naturalistically represented but seemed, like the head, to be moulded in bronze. The Old Shepherd bears some resemblance to the traditional Greek mask of a satyr, but with curly fringes of wool; we wanted to suggest that he had become like one of his own sheep.

Huge quantities of clay and plaster of Paris were delivered to the Property Department and gradually the room became crowded with clay heads swathed in damp cloths. Almost daily we were asked to compare the sketches with the newly-modelled heads before the clay hardened. Once the plaster casts were taken and the leather pressed firmly into the greased moulds, it would have been unreasonable to ask for an alteration in style or size. This, however, happened in one case. The Man from Corinth, when he came out of the mould, surprised us with a cruel, mean expression, and had to be rebuilt on kinder, more benign lines.

THE MAN FROM CORINTH

It could be seen at an early stage that the thirty-three masks could not possibly be ready for rehearsal, and this presented another problem. The process of modelling and making masks is of necessity a slow one, although somewhat speeded up by a specially contrived drying tent fitted with powerful lamps. It was essential for the actors to become accustomed not only to wearing masks but to seeing on each other the expressions they could achieve by tilting, bowing or raising their heads. The Property Department decided to divert some of its time and attention to making papier mâché replicas of the masks, with a cartoon suggestion of hair painted in sepia, no time being wasted on colouring, or on 'mocking-up' wigs and beards.

129

As the play took shape day by day these pale grey faces became familiar to us all while the work progressed in the Property Shop. Actors were called for frequent, long, and troublesome fittings which were conducted in a most amiable manner; and, considering the hot summer weather, this showed remarkable tact and co-operation on the part of all concerned. Jacqueline Cundall prepared the way with the utmost confidence.

It is perhaps not easy to realize how much tact is required mutually of actors, designers and technicians at fittings. The actor is inevitably over-conscious of what he considers his own physical short-comings. Moreover there is always a discrepancy between the image of his 'character' which has formed in his imagination and the image which confronts him in the fitting-room looking glass. Sometimes the surprise is a pleasant one; but it is still a surprise. It is not mere vanity which makes an actor fussy at fittings. The clothes are an essential part of the character he will present. They must not only look right, they must feel right. Likewise, the designer is apt to be anxious that the designed garments should suit and please the wearer, and that the design should show to advantage on the stage. This can only be so if it is worn with appropriate style. Both parties, then, have to be careful not to allow ruffled feelings to be transferred to the tailor, and not to blame the maker for what may be faults of design or the actor's inability to wear the dress with an air.

Opera singers, trained to use their ears but not their eyes, are the designer's bane. Hats designed for the back of the head will be pressed down onto the bridge of the nose; it is nothing for an opera singer to put on a dress back to front, to omit essential parts of a costume, or to add little personal touches, a bow here or a frill there, an Aberdeen terrier in brilliants pinned to the front of a medieval wimple. We both know an opera chorister who used habitually to appear at matinées of *Madame Butterfly* wearing a thick tweed coat and skirt under her kimono. She did this in order to have time to get home between matinée and evening performances to give her aged mother her tea. Not unreasonably, this seemed to her important, and the fact that she looked to the audience like the wrath of God worried her not at all. But also not unreasonably, it worried the designer very much.

At fittings tact on the part of the designer often has to verge on hypocrisy. A dumpy person with a short thick neck cannot always be truthfully told why his collar is designed in a certain style, or why the lines of the dress tend to be vertical not horizontal. If he has any sense, he will realize. But too few of us have any sense, and too many of us have no dispassionate idea whatever of our own appearance. The handsomest and best built are often the most acutely conscious of inferiority; the gawkiest and plainest specimens are frequently, and mercifully, convinced that they are Venus or Adonis.

Always it must be remembered that the design is nothing without the co-operation of its makers. The morale of the wardrobe staff is no less important than that of the company. It is the director's duty to make every actor, from the leading man down to the humblest understudy, feel that he is making a contribution that is not only indispensable but valued; similarly the designer must see that every member of the wardrobe staff, from the chief cutter down to the little middle-aged lady who sits at a machine and runs up the very plainest seams for petticoats, is credited for good work and allowed to feel an indispensable part of an essentially co-operative effort.

But again the design for a dress is nothing without the co-operation of its wearer. If the wearer is not given confidence, does not feel happy and easy in the dress, then

ANTIGONE

the dress is a failure. An excellent design can be ruined if its wearer has caught in the mirror a glance of despair, even a flicker of anxiety, pass between the designer and the cutter. That is why the atmosphere of fittings is important. There need be no gross flattery, but it is vital that there be an air of mutual consideration and respect, and a mutual confidence that all will be well. That is why, in the particular context of these masks, we feel grateful to Miss Cundall for her air of unwavering self-confidence and calm, and to the actors for being gay and co-operative in the early stages of fittings when the masks looked ridiculous and felt uncomfortable. The whole experiment absolutely depended upon their agreeing to co-operate in a plan which seemed likely at best to eclipse their personalities, and at worst to make them look absolute fools.

At Stratford the actors made light of the inevitable discomfort of covering their faces, and appreciated the plans made for their clear seeing, hearing and speaking. Inside the leather mask there was a perspex head-band, which, resting on the actor's brows, tilted the mask so that it fitted as nearly as possible against the contours of the human face. After the beards and stylized wigs had been made and fitted, the masks were painted with subtle shading to stress the planes and angles, in the colours and tones representing wood or metal as planned in the sketches.

At the final fitting, when the draped hood matching

SCALE = Mask + wig larger than life

Bronze & shining with verdigris – green high lights.

Colour NOT indicated here.

Cunning eyes

the costume was fixed to the top of the mask, there was a feeling of wonder that the actor's personality was not submerged but, in a strange way, enhanced. It made one realize that human personality is not so exclusively expressed in the face as one is apt to suppose. The posture and rhythm of each figure remained entirely characteristic; and the expressionless quality of the mask emphasized all other means of expression. Incidentally, we found that those immobile masks gave to a listening figure an intensity which more mobile features never seem to achieve.

Wig & beard leaf-shaped — Crown of bays removable, put on Oedipus' crown for final scene

Of course, it is not suggested that masks would be suitable for the kind of acting in which subtle and constantly changing shades of expression are required—such acting as is called for by the plays of Shakespeare or of Chekhov—but where a powerful simplicity is demanded the most obvious drawback of the mask becomes an asset.

THE DÉCOR

Now with heads and hair and faces so far removed from realism, it was out of all question that bare hands should be seen. A member of the Chorus whose face appeared to be carved out of teak or olive, whose frame, heavily padded across the shoulders, bespoke a dejected infirmity, in whose gait was seen the palsied tottering of extremest eld, could hardly thrust out of his sleeves the plump pink paw of a vigorous man of thirty. The sleeves had to be looped and draped over gloves carefully but inconspicuously painted to match the dress. In more extreme cases, more extreme hands were called for. The most spectacular were for Tiresias who, it was planned, should have bird-like claws. The fact that they took on a crustaceous aspect was by the way. The old Priest was given long bony fingers which matched his ivory dome. Jocasta and Oedipus were planned in silver and gold. It was found that Oedipus needed two pairs of hands. The first, long-nailed and golden-fingered, was encrusted with gold rings; the second was ringless for the final scene when the golden mask was veiled.

Now it began to be apparent that the décor would have to have the courage of its convictions, that masked actors, some of them in shoes with soles six inches thick, would have their freedom of expression very severely limited. How would all this work?

Let us take the play step by step and endeavour to suggest some of its meanings and how we interpreted these meaning in terms of practical stagecraft.

The scene is Thebes. One deduces an entrance to the palace and access from a city which can, with symbolic advantage, be imagined below, at the foot of a rock on which the royal residence, half palace, half fortress, is founded. An altar is required; the statues of Athena, Dionysus and Apollo may be inferred. For all this the stage at Stratford was reasonably suitable. It permitted no literal suggestion of locality but did, we thought, sufficiently suggest an entrance to a palace of no identifiable date or style. It was insufficiently large, ominous, majestic; not exactly right but not, we believed, obtrusively wrong. There were excellent entrances from below; the whereabouts of Delphi and Cithaeron could be sufficiently indicated; an altar could be simply contrived. For statues of deities we had no room, nor were we anxious to juxtapose them with what we hoped would be the monumental and sculptured-looking figures of the actors. The altar was to be supposed that of Apollo. Other deities must be vaguely and not specifically addressed.

The play opens with a processional entrance of the mourning inhabitants of plague-stricken Thebes. They come to invoke, through an aged Priest who is their spokesman, the help of Oedipus in discovering the cause of the pestilence.

The suppliant citizens wore shapeless dresses of very dark grey, mottled with black and dark blue and brown; their faces were covered with flat masks of gauze, like those of a surgeon at an operation. The idea was that these figures should be totally anonymous, unidentifiable as to age, sex or stature. Four of the suppliants carried huge bowls of incense; the remaining thirty-six carried long, gaunt, pale grey branches to which were tied wisps of wool in white and grey, the traditional emblems of supplication. The Priest was a tiny figure in dead black with an emaciated bone-coloured face and very long bony fingers. The lights were very dim; from the incense bowls thick smoke curled upward. It was intended that through the smoke almost nothing should be visible but the wool-hung branches of the suppliants, some as much as eight feet high, slowly invading and surrounding the entrance to the palace.

Then the Chorus entered down stairs on either side of the palace, fifteen old men in varying tones, not pale, not dark, of earth colours—grey, sepia, umber. Then guards in black and grey with lead-coloured masks and enormously long spears. Then, last of all, alone and from the palace, Oedipus, toweringly large, in gold.

All this occurred in absolute silence, and very slowly, with the smoke from the incense wreathing and curling and obscuring all detail, so that the effect of the masks upon an unaccustomed audience was very gradual. Our

135

hope was that by the time the King began to speak the audience might already be inclined to accept the masks, already be inclined to accept the slow processional movement, already be inclined to look for symbols, not realism, be prepared for speech that was not an imitation of 'real' conversation, but the incantation of a ritual.

The long speech by the aged Priest, which opens the play, was very skilfully delivered by the actor to establish a convention of highly stylized declamation from which no one departed all evening. But at the same time, within this highly artificial framework he contrived the greatest possible variety of pitch and tempo and, while making its literal meaning clear, gave the speech an overall musical shape. It was, in fact, treated as an operatic aria.

At the same time the choreography endeavoured to establish the convention of movement to which the audience would be asked to subscribe: a movement at all times governed by the music of the spoken word, a movement in which each actor expressed himself individually within

an overall symphonic pattern. In the opening aria we tried to help the audience to expect movement which, while mostly very slow, would also by realistic standards be very exaggerated. For instance, instead of kneeling in supplication to the King, the Priest lay absolutely prostrate. The supporting counter-point of choral supplication was equally broad. One gentleman, whose mask and figure suggested that he was about a hundred and ten years old, lay on his back, head downwards on the staircase. Other goings-on

PRIEST

were no less extreme. This extremity was the inevitable consequence of the décor, which was itself so strong that merely life-sized acting would have been completely swamped.

Whether all this achieved much of its intention, one can never tell. The intention was to remove the play completely from the area of theatrical naturalism, and to compel the audience to relate what they were seeing and hearing to their religious experience; at the same time to accustom the audience to sights and sounds so unfamiliar that if unprepared they would be extremely distracting and probably get laughs. Above all, the attempt was to raise the tragedy from the triviality of detail and particularity, on to the plane where it belongs, of abstracted and remote grandeur. The exact details of the story of What Happened to Poor Mr. A. and Mrs. B. may be interesting and deeply touching, but insofar as they are just details and insofar as Mr. A. and Mrs. B. are just individuals, the story remains on the level of journalism, remains bourgeois, our interest remains on the level of gossip and the emotion aroused is not tragic but pathetic. Tragedy presupposes the abstraction of Mr. A. from Main Street, of Mrs. B. from the washline and the sink, and our own abstraction with them from the trivialities of day to day, from what the very word 'journalism' denotes. The performance of a tragedy must aim higher than at an audience's susceptibility to pathos. An audience will cry readily; the death of Little Willie or a pretty girl singing the sorriest rubbish will melt to tender tears the hardest-bitten men and the hardest biting women. The emotion aroused by even a half-decent performance of great tragedy cannot be measured in terms of chewed hankies and misted specs. The full impact of great tragedy is not immediate; it takes effect slowly. It lies in wait on the fringe of dreams. It

wakes one with a start in the small hours. It can shake
the confident and strengthen the weak, stop the clock,
roll back the seas. It can give a new meaning to life,
and an old meaning to death.

THE COURSE OF THE PLAY

FOLLOWING THE PRIEST'S SPEECH, Oedipus promises the
Thebans to do all that he can to investigate the cause
of the plague, and reminds them that he has already sent
his wife's brother, Creon, to consult the Oracle of Apollo
at Delphi.

Creon returns with the news that to heal itself of the
pestilence Thebes must drive out a defiling thing. The
defilement is connected with the mysterious disappearance
some years before of King Laius. Laius had been the
predecessor of Oedipus on the throne of Thebes. Jocasta,
now wife of Oedipus, had formerly been the wife of
Laius.

The scene is full of facts; it 'plants' the whole domestic
and dynastic situation; it puts the audience in possession
of the facts of Laius' mysterious disappearance and suggests that these facts are important. On the emotional
side it establishes a situation of some tension between
Oedipus and Creon. On the philosophic side it immediately establishes that the dramatist is not going to accord
unqualified reverence to the Delphic oracle and the cult
of Apollo. Creon's first line, 'Pain turns to pleasure,
when we have set the crooked straight' is so broadly and
emphatically Delphic in style that we do not doubt that
the author's intention is satirical. The satire is the more
marked because Creon's entrance has been so strongly
prepared. The audience is keyed up to receive important
and interesting news, and is then offered this caricature
of Delphic utterance. Of course Oedipus and all on the

stage take it *au grand sérieux*; the audience, however, is expected to be more sceptical.

It is a point we think insufficiently stressed by commentators that Creon brings the oracle, unsupported by written confirmation, and, furthermore, that it is Creon, not Delphi, who suggests that the defilement might be connected with the disappearance of Laius. If the play were to be interpreted on a naturalistic level, like a detective story, this might well be taken as a clue to the fact that the oracle should not be regarded by Oedipus, also that Creon is not a trustworthy fellow. It is a nice point whether, in this play, Sophocles intends to suggest the tyrant which Creon later became. We regarded it as an irrelevant issue and tried, like Delphi, to be ambiguously vague, showing Creon neither in a sympathetic nor an unsympathetic light.

The scene was played in a rapid, business-like key, with Oedipus perplexed, anxious, and Creon confident, assured and dominant. The mask of Creon, in bronze, was meant to suggest a face cunning, watchful and inscrutable.

Left alone, the Chorus invokes Apollo, Athena and Dionysus to drive out the god of Death and Pestilence. This chorus we tried to make as lyrical as we could, with the voices moving gradually nearer and nearer to song and a choreography, expressive of supplication and adoration, moving gradually from individual expression towards a unified dance. The intention was to give the audience a complete change both for the eye and ear— a different feeling, different rhythm, different colour of sound, sustained and emotional melody after a scene of business-like prose, complex but slow movement after stillness. It was designed as a bridge to carry the audience from the prosaic and 'plotty' scene with Creon to a mysterious and ironic scene of ritual, the scene of Oedipus' curse on the murderer whom the audience already suspects to be himself.

When the King reappeared after this chorus he carried a great golden sceptre ornamented with a golden trefoil. He knelt at the altar and laid his sceptre symbolically before the god during the passage where he dedicates himself to the search for the murderer. In every way the Chorus displays fear of this curse and respect and admiration for their King—not the attitude of men towards a fellow-man, but a superstitious and adoring reverence mixed with cunning and fear, the attitude of men towards a powerful and capricious god. Our aim was to suggest that to the Chorus, representing ordinary citizens, this *was* a manifestation of god, of wisdom and light made manifest, about whom they felt 'In thy light shall we see light'.

Hard upon the King's curse comes the entrance of the prophet, Tiresias. The seer is blind. The apostle of the god of light is dark. Then, later, as a result of enlightenment as to his own identity, Oedipus dashes out the light of his own eyes. The symbolism of all this seemed to us to be extremely near the heart of the play's mystery. It also seemed that, just as Delphi is presented in quite a satirical light, so is the portrait of Tiresias by no means flattering. He seems to embody the soul of superstition which we all fear and of which we are all ashamed, and which, with all our shame, we cannot quite dismiss.

The figure of the prophet, then, had to suggest emphatically blindness, literally obscurantism, ferocity and intransigence. He evidently inspired awe and terror not only in the Thebans but in Oedipus as well. We wanted to make a derogatory comment upon this feeling, to imply that it was superstition rather than justified reverence,

140

by making the figure not only formidable but squalid and a little absurd.

The prophet wore white—dead white—the first time this colour had appeared. His head was that of a sort of blind and featherless bird, also dead white, a great beak between two black eyeless sockets. The hair resembled feathers. The hands and the feet were slightly feathered. The hem of the dress was torn and stained. From the scraggy neck of this apparition there depended an enormous necklace of broken eggshells. We made no attempt to depict the legendary bi-sexuality of Tiresias, but attempted only to suggest a terrifying being of incredible age who had studied, lived, loved and feared the birds so long and so deeply that at last he had become a sort of bird.

The scene with Tiresias was played with a great deal of violent movement and shouting. Tragic dignity and nobility were thrown to the winds. The prophet raved and screamed, took an epileptic fit, fell headlong down steps. The King was shown to be touched to the quick by the hints and accusations. He too screamed in a fury of fear and rage. The Chorus reacted no less violently to the abandoned and wild passions of the great ones. It was played at a galloping speed except for a heavily marked moment when Oedipus asks, 'Who was my father?' Then again, at the end, there was a long, slow passage of silent mime after the prophet had gone, when Oedipus for the first time realizes that he *may* be defiled, that the net *may* be closing around him, and when the old men of Thebes, battered by the events of the scene, refuse to look at their King, shrink from his touch, allow him to see that the prophet's words have taken some root in their hearts. Then Oedipus withdrew, manifestly shaken to the core.

The Chorus drew together and expressed the horror of

TIRESIAS

decent, conventional people confronted with something they regard as monstrous, not to be spoken of, not to be thought of. This chorus, a terse and powerful condensation of the original, is in Yeats' finest frenzy; the fifteen men who played the Chorus at Stratford performed it with extraordinary effect—a steady *crescendo* and *accelerando* from a slow whisper of fear to a rapid bellow of bourgeois hate and defiance, a really formidable exhibition of the little man at bay, the worm turning, conventional goodness baring its savage fangs.

Right on top of this Creon entered like a clap of thunder, scattering the Chorus from the stage. The scene between Creon and Oedipus was conducted in a series of sharp *crescendos* each coming to a climax, mounting at last to full power on the invocation of Thebes and the entrance of the Queen.

Here, as again and again, it is apparent that the form of this tragedy is far nearer to opera than to the conventional 'naturalistic' play of today. This scene is a great duet for tenor and bass. What is said is only partly adequate if divorced from a more powerful musical form than 'natural' conversation.

Paradoxically, it was in the passages of stichomythia, the single line speeches, that the Yeats' version proved least adequate. The great speeches of declamation, so we thought, were effective in their stark simplicity. It was the short, sharp dialogue exchanges which lacked form. They were clear, aristocratic, but they did not chime and ring and move forward on the twin impulse, which is not only logical but musical.

It is noticeable that the anger of Oedipus with Creon is not rational. Creon speaks and behaves reasonably; Oedipus does not. The explanation offered to Jocasta, to explain his rage, is a transparently feeble rationalization. The anger of Oedipus, we believe, arises from feel-

143

ings of guilt and fear provoked by his formidable encounter with Tiresias.

The 'Commos', (or in operatic parlance, Ensemble for Principals and Chorus) which follows the quarrel between Creon and Oedipus, has been omitted by Yeats. This seemed to us to ruin an indispensable musical transition. Borrowing heavily from other translations, we put back this Ensemble, as a bridge which led from the tumult and agitation of the quarrel to the calm of the great scene of recollection between Jocasta and Oedipus.

Incidentally, this short bridge faced the Chorus with its most exacting technical problem of the performance. The final choral lines had to be spoken *rallentando* and *diminuendo*, while at the same time each member of the Chorus moved backwards from the stage, separating himself from his fellows. It is always hard for a Chorus to keep in unison on a *rallentando* rhythm; the difficulty was immensely increased by having to separate in space, while holding together in rhythm and feeling.

OEDIPUS AND JOCASTA

OEDIPUS NOW RECALLS a series of events from his early life. In terms of dramatic construction it may at a first glance seem odd that these facts, which it is essential for the audience to hear, should be recapitulated to his wife. But, of course, this is highly significant. Jocasta must be supposed to be hearing them for the first time. Oedipus has not hitherto been able to confide these particular memories even to her. They have, to use one of the psychological technical terms which cannot in this context be avoided, been repressed. Sophocles has been at pains to suggest that the recollection is wrung out of Oedipus as the result of shock, and that it is dredged up from the depths of his being. The whole scene is a confession, with Jocasta in the role of priest, Oedipus as penitent. It is also strikingly like a psychological analysis, with Jocasta as doctor, Oedipus as patient. There is, further, a marked suggestion of a child 'owning up' to Mother.

Although much of its detail is not relevant to the specific question of design and the visual impression of the play, nevertheless it was from consideration of this scene that our whole idea of the play's interpretation originated. The scene is so crucial to any interpretation of the play that it must be discussed in some detail. Therefore we quote the Yeats' text:

Jocasta: In the name of the Gods, King, what put you in anger?

Oedipus: I will tell you; for I honour you more than these men do. The cause is Creon and his plots against me.

Jocasta: Speak on, if you can tell clearly how this quarrel arose.

Oedipus: He says that I am guilty of the blood of Laius.

Jocasta: On his own knowledge, or on hearsay?

Oedipus: He has made a rascal of a seer his mouthpiece.

Jocasta: Do not fear that there is truth in what he says. Listen to me, and learn to your comfort that nothing born of woman can know what is to come. I will give you proof of that. An oracle came to Laius once, I will not say from Phoebus, but from his ministers, that he was doomed to die by the hand of his own child sprung from him and me. When his child was but three days old, Laius bound its feet together and had it thrown by sure hands upon a trackless mountain; and when Laius was murdered at the place where three highways meet, it was, or so at least the rumour says, by foreign robbers. So Apollo did not bring it about that the child should kill its father, nor did Laius die in the dreadful way he feared by his child's hand. Yet that was how the message of the seers mapped out the future. Pay no attention to such things. What the God

145

would show he will need no help to show it,
but bring it to light himself.

Oedipus: What restlessness of soul, lady, has come upon
me since I heard you speak, what a tumult of
the mind!

Jocasta: What is this new anxiety? What has startled
you?

Oedipus: You said that Laius was killed where three
highways meet.

Jocasta: Yes: that was the story.

Oedipus: And where is the place?

Jocasta: In Phocis where the road divides branching off
to Delphi and to Daulia.

Oedipus: And when did it happen? How many years ago?

Jocasta: News was published in this town just before you
came into power.

Oedipus: O Zeus! What have you planned to do unto me?

Jocasta: He was tall; the silver had just come into his
hair; and in shape not greatly unlike to you.

Oedipus: Unhappy that I am! It seems that I have laid a
dreadful curse upon myself, and did not know it.

Jocasta: What do you say? I tremble when I look on you,
my King.

Oedipus: And I have a misgiving that the seer can see
indeed. But I will know it all more clearly, if
you tell me one thing more.

Jocasta: Indeed, though I tremble I will answer whatever
you ask.

Oedipus: Had he but a small troop with him; or did he
travel like a great man with many followers?

Jocasta: There were but five in all—one of them a
herald; and there was one carriage with Laius
in it.

Oedipus: Alas! It is now clear indeed. Who was it brought
the news, lady?

Jocasta: A servant—the one survivor.

Oedipus: Is he by chance in the house now?

Jocasta: No; for when he found you reigning instead of
Laius he besought me, his hand clasped in mine,
to send him to the fields among the cattle that
he might be far from the sight of this town; and

146

	I sent him. He was a worthy man for a slave and might have asked a bigger thing.
Oedipus:	I would have him return to us without delay.
Jocasta:	Oedipus, it is easy. But why do you ask this?
Oedipus:	I fear that I have said too much, and therefore I would question him.
Jocasta:	He shall come, but I too have a right to know what lies so heavy upon your heart, my King.
Oedipus:	Yes: and it shall not be kept from you now that my fear has grown so heavy. Nobody is more to me than you, nobody has the same right to learn my good or evil luck. My father was Polybius of Corinth, my mother the Dorian Merope, and I was held the foremost man in all that town until a thing happened—a thing to startle a man, though not to make him angry as it made me. We were sitting at the table, and a man who had drunk too much cried out that I was not my father's son—and I, though angry, restrained my anger for that day; but the next day went to my father and my mother and questioned them. They were indignant at the taunt and that comforted me—and yet the man's words rankled, for they had spread a rumour through the town. Without consulting my father or my mother I went to Delphi, but Phoebus told me nothing of the thing for which I came, but much of other things—things of sorrow and of terror: that I should live in incest with my mother, and beget a brood that men would shudder to look upon; that I should be my father's murderer. Hearing those words I fled out of Corinth, and from that day have but known where it lies when I have found its direction by the stars. I sought where I might escape those infamous things—the doom that was laid upon me. I came in my flight to that very spot where you tell me this king perished. Now, lady, I will tell you the truth. When I had come close up to those three roads, I came upon a herald, and a man like him you have described seated

in a carriage. The man who held the reins and the old man himself would not give me room, but thought to force me from the path, and I struck the driver in my anger. The old man, seeing what I had done, waited till I was passing him and then struck me upon the head. I paid him back in full, for I knocked him out of the carriage with a blow of my stick. He rolled on his back, and after that I killed them all. If this stranger were indeed Laius, is there a more miserable man in the world than the man before you? Is there a man more hated of Heaven? No stranger, no citizen, may receive him into his house, not a soul may speak to him, and no mouth but my own mouth has laid this curse upon me. Am I not wretched? May I be swept from this world before I have endured this doom!

The shock of the Tiresias scene, then of the quarrel with Creon, is now capped for Oedipus by the dreadful intimations of Jocasta's speech about the death of Laius. 'I have a right to know,' says Jocasta, 'what lies so heavy on your heart.' 'Yes,' Oedipus replies, 'and it shall not be kept from you now that my fear has grown so heavy.' The reiterated 'heavy' is Yeats, not Sophocles. It is indicative that Yeats too saw this as a confessional scene, saw Oedipus as a penitent longing to shed a heavy load of guilt.

Again, when halfway through the great speech, Oedipus approaches the hard core of his repression, he says, 'Now, lady, I will tell you the truth.' Does not this suggest that between the husband and wife there had been not merely concealment but prevarication?

Next notice how many of the incidentals of the story are symbolic. The detail is not mere decoration to make the story more picturesque. It is very carefully and consciously selected to set certain ideas in train by the power of association. Now it is obviously a mistake to try and

148

label a symbol with a precise or definitive meaning. If the author wished to be precise or definitive he would not be using symbols. Nevertheless, it may be of some interest to suggest some of the possible symbolic associations attached to some of the details of the encounter of Oedipus and Laius, provided it is always understood that such associations and their interpretation are essentially subjective. Each of us is entitled to make his own interpretation. By speaking symbolically and not in direct matter-of-fact tones the author deliberately asks each interpreter to use his own imagination.

We quote our own interpretations, therefore, not as being in any sense authoritative, but simply because the interpretation of this remarkable series of symbols led us to conclusions about the meaning of the play, and thence to practical decision in the matter of production.

First, Oedipus is speaking. He is the 'I' of the narrative. The symbols are presented as occurring to his consciousness. Nevertheless Oedipus is himself a symbolic figure. He stands, we believe, for Man in general, for each one of us in particular. Therefore, in interpreting the symbols of the scene we must think not only, What might this or that represent to Oedipus? but rather, What does this or that represent to me?

The dominant figure in this murder story is its victim —Laius, the Father. Here let us momentarily diverge to reflect how the figure of the Murdered Father haunted the consciousness and the sub-consciousness of Shakespeare. The Murdered Father dominates *Hamlet*; the Murdered King who is a symbolic father of his subjects, or, in psychological parlance, a father figure, dominates *Macbeth*, dominates *Julius Caesar*. While Lear is not literally murdered by Regan and Goneril, he is a figure of the Destroyed Father—it is parricide at one remove.

Now let us consider how Sophocles presents this father

figure. He is described: tall, like Oedipus in shape, his hair beginning to whiten. Compare the description of Hamlet's father: 'his beard a sable silvered'. The intention evidently is to present a majestic figure, not young, but not old, and to insist on the likeness to Oedipus, the likeness to the 'I' of the story.

The emphasis upon Laius is the more marked because of the complete lack of emphasis upon the adoptive parents Polybus and Merope. They are presented without character of any kind.

Corinth is presented without detail except that the rumour which alarmed Oedipus was provoked by a drunken man at a feast. Is not this episode intended to exemplify the great part played by chance or luck, or even by Apollo, in human affairs? If it had not been for a chance word by a babbling drunkard thrown by chance in his way, Oedipus need never have known he was not the real son of Polybus and Merope. Unlucky chance, or a calculating predestinating Apollo, brought him face to face with Laius at a narrow pass, took him to Thebes of all the many cities he might have gone to, taught him the lucky answer to the Sphinx, rewarded him with the hand of Jocasta.

After learning he was not the son of the ruler of Corinth, Oedipus sought advice from Delphi. The answer, that he would kill his real father and be husband to his real mother, was so shocking that he fled from Delphi by night, in a darkness symbolic of terror, mystery, confusion and immensity. Corinth thereafter was but an image, discernible by starlight—no longer ever to be in the rational, daylit, everyday world.

'Now, lady, I will tell you the truth.' And here suddenly the matter of whereabouts becomes significant and symbolic—a crossroads, a crux, a place of decision. It was at a crossroads, and with some of the same symbolic overtones, that Peer Gynt met Destiny in the person of Button Moulder.

Sophocles has been at pains to 'plant' the importance of this place where three ways meet. It is repeatedly mentioned. The ways divide to Delphi and to Daulia. Delphi would seem to suggest what many psychologists believe the Left Hand, movements or turnings to the left, implies in dreams, a movement away from consciousness, away from rationality. Daulia, therefore, we suppose, implies a Right Hand turn, in the direction of commonsense.

As well, however, as being a place of decision, the place where three ways meet can also be regarded as a symbol of another kind. We asked a psychiatrist how he would interpret this symbol if it occurred in the dream of a patient. His reply, quite unbiased by the context which was not revealed to him until after he had answered the question, was this: To the primitive mind this symbol would immediately suggest the place where the trunk meets the legs, the 'fork' of the human body.

Oedipus encounters Laius, then, in a place of decision, and a place where, in physiological terms, the organs of sex are situated. The locality is further described in terms which seem to confirm the sexual symbolism. In one of the invocatory speeches at the end of the play Oedipus cries, 'O three roads, O secret glen, O coppice and narrow way where three roads met; you that drank up the blood I spilt, the blood was my own, my father's blood.' That is the Yeats version. Gilbert Murray's confirms the analogy: 'O Crossing of the Roads, O secret glen and dusk of crowding woods, O narrow footpath creeping to the brink where meet the Three. I gave you blood to drink. Do ye remember? 'Twas my life-blood hot from my own father's heart.' Sheppard translates:

O ye three roads, O secret mountain-glen,
Trees, and a pathway narrowed to the place
Where met the three, do you remember me?
I gave you blood to drink, my father's blood,
And so my own.

And Jebb: 'O ye three roads, and thou secret glen—
thou coppice and narrow way where three paths meet—
ye who drank from my hands that father's blood which
was mine own.'

The evidence is hard to gainsay that the meeting of
the three ways is itself an image of the meeting of the
three lives of Laius, Oedipus and Jocasta, and that the
physical description is a veiled but unmistakable allusion
to the female anatomy.

Now notice that the father figure is described as seated
in a carriage. His powers in the eyes of the son are 'extended'. Means of transport with their attributes of speed
and mobility are well-known symbols of power. Every
young child longs nowadays for a bicycle, where in another generation it longed for a pony. The longed-for
extension once obtained, it is immediately turned in the
child's imagination into a still more powerful extension
of personality; the bicycle becomes an imaginary horse,
or railway engine (the iron horse of the nineteenth century), or car, or aeroplane (the winged horse of the
twentieth century). And to the normal child these
power-symbols are associated with its father. The kitchen,
and all that therein is, belongs to Mummy, the source of
nutriment and cosiness; the car, with its associations of
power, speed, adventure, is Daddy's.

The fact that Laius is mounted on a carriage enhances
the image of Laius as a powerful father figure. When
Oedipus meets him and disputes the possession of this
highly significant passage, it is not just one man meeting

another. The foot passenger, though younger and there-fore probably stronger, is at a tremendous disadvantage.

What are we to make of the two subsidiary figures, the two servants of Laius, one of whom is described as a 'herald'? Was he one of the five attendants upon Laius, similar to the Five-Wits of the English morality play? It is possible that in earlier lost versions of the story Laius was so accompanied. In that case one might interpret the Herald as the faculty of speech.

In the Yeats version it is made clear that Laius struck the first blow; but Yeats omits the fact that he struck with what Murray translates 'his iron-branched goad', and Sheppard as 'his forking goad', and Jebb 'his goad with two teeth'. Sophocles makes the two men strike each other with instruments that may not unreasonably be regarded as phallic symbols. The battle is analogous to that between two stags who fight for supremacy of the herd.

Finally, Oedipus, in an access of irrational fury, not content with the destruction of Laius, kills all the ser-vants. This suggests that in Father Murder one killing is not enough; all the attendants on the father figure must be killed as well. Compare in *Macbeth* the destruc-tion of the two sleeping grooms in the chamber next to Duncan. The same idea occurs in *Julius Caesar* when the conspirators, in planning the murder of Caesar, wonder whether Antony must not be removed too. An-tony is described as a limb of the trunk whose head is Caesar.

RELIGIOUS AND DRAMATIC RITUAL

OUR PRODUCTION WAS NOT AIMING to persuade the audi-ence that the goings-on on the stage were really happen-ing, nor to attempt to induce illusion, but rather to make the audience participate in a ritual.

153

It was true, we realized, that the story of Oedipus would not be as familiar to an audience in Canada in 1955 as to an Athenian audience two thousand years earlier. But the story is extremely interesting and extremely lucidly unfolded by Sophocles. The important thing, it seemed, was that the large majority of our audience *would* be familiar with the idea of ritual re-enactment of a Saviour's Passion. It should be possible to make clear the analogy between religious and dramatic ritual, and in a manner to convince any reasonable person that the attempt was serious, respectable and untainted by sectarianism or blasphemy.

The Passion of Oedipus, we assumed, was a symbol of experiences which all human beings are compelled to undergo. To suffer with Oedipus, to partake of this Communion, the audience must be prepared to enter into a world of symbols exactly analogous to the experience of dreaming.

In dreams, the images and events of everyday are replaced by symbols arranged in patterns which do not correspond to those of everyday life. For instance, in a dream one can be simultaneously indoors and out; one can in the same dream-context encounter the living and the dead, sometimes those long dead. In a dream one can undergo astounding and terrifying experiences in perfect calm, or be alarmed by apparently insignificant trifles.

Now dream-experience is subject to interpretation. It is possible by meditation and concentration, and after a little experience, to know with some degree of certainty what this or that symbol represents in terms of waking experience. In exactly analogous manner can the experience of Oedipus and the spectators' sympathetic experience when the tragedy is acted before them, be related to that of everyday.

But, just as a dream can be profoundly affecting even when uninterpreted, or misinterpreted, so, we hoped, could an adequate performance of this tragedy. It might make a mysterious and even baffling impression upon many people who could not, or would not, bother to interpret its symbols. Nevertheless, the story is so strong, and corresponds to something so deep in our being, that the impression, though baffling, could hardly be negligible. Very few people, we believed, could see it without feeling that for an hour or two they had been in contact with a world no more unintelligible and far more cohesive and significant than the impression each of us constructs for himself of the real world, the world of everyday waking experience.

In terms of the stage, the scene between Oedipus and Jocasta seemed to demand stillness and concentration, the more so as it follows the *allegro agitato* of the quarrel with Creon. Oedipus stood with Jocasta's hand on his brow. The actor suggested that the long speech of recollection was delivered almost in a state of trance. When he reached the words, 'Now, lady, I will tell you the truth', he suggested, with deep and struggling breaths, a lapse into deeper trance; when the description of the murder was reached it was spoken in a fury of recollected passion. The words, 'And then I killed them all', were accompanied by a pantomime of indiscriminate violence. After that there was a long pause. The actor seemed to emerge from his trance and the speech was finished in a far calmer and more rational tone.

A BREAK IN THE ACTION

AFTER THE KING AND QUEEN WITHDREW to the palace the Chorus gave utterance to sentiments which in Yeats' version satirize the smugness of church-going conventionality and the attitude of those who hope by behaving well in school to deserve a handsome prize from the Headmaster in the hereafter.

Regretfully we must confess that the humorous and satiric aspects, both in this chorus and elsewhere in the play, were utterly missed in this production. We were aware that this bitter humour pervades the play, even in its last tremendous lines. But we could see no way of expressing this that did not border too closely on triviality and an unseasonable flippancy. It is a confession of second-rateness. In the greatest tragedy humour is always present, just as great comedy is always shot through with sadness. An evening in the theatre of high but humourless intention is like a dinner without a sweet, meat followed by more meat and then a draught of strong and bitter coffee.

When Jocasta returns from the palace her mood is one of desperate anxiety. Gone is the former scepticism in which she bade Oedipus pay no attention to oracles and divination. The panic of Oedipus has infected her. Publicly and ceremoniously she beseeches Apollo to cleanse her city, her family and herself from pollution. Apollo, as Gilbert Murray has pointed out, means to destroy Jocasta, not to save her. Her prayer is interrupted by the arrival of the Man from Corinth, which seems like a deliverance but is really a link in the chain of destruction.

At this point—the arrival of the Man from Corinth —we broke the continuity of the play by a ten-minute intermission. Such a transgression of the author's intention was certainly not made without careful consideration. Two principal reasons governed the decision. First, the conditions of the Canadian summer and of the particular theatre for which this production was designed are such that a breath of fresh air is almost a physical necessity after about an hour in the theatre. It must be remembered that though the climate in Greece is hot too, the Dionysiac Festival occurred in the spring, not in high summer; and, more important, the audience sat in the open air. It should also be remembered that the Greek audience witnessed a performance of a familiar story in a familiar style. The audiences at Stratford were required, we believe, to make a no less stern effort of concentration and, at the same time, a considerable effort of intellectual, religious and emotional adaptation to ideas which were not in the least familiar. This led on to the second consideration: if both performers and audience were adequately to stay the course and give to the second half of the evening the same concentration as to the first, a rest and a breath of air were essential.

Why, it may be asked, should the power of endurance of a modern audience in Canada be so much less than that of an Athenian audience two thousand years ago? The question is not hard to answer. The Athenian audience was predominantly local and belonged predominantly to a class of society which had plenty of help to do the bread-winning and domestic chores. One has always to bear in mind that the glory that was Greece was not achieved without the assistance of slave labour. The Athenian Festival was a great religious occasion and its audience was not only in duty and reverence bound to give its entire energies and attention to the performance, but was literally free from other and more mundane preoccupations.

In contrast, the great majority of our audience was heavily burdened by daily cares—office appointments, feeding of stock, baby-sitting, and the like. Many had come a long journey and would have another long journey after the performance before they got to their beds. Above all, our performance was being given in a locality and an epoch which had entirely lost the tradition of regarding Art in general, or the Theatre in particular, as being in the realm of religion or even as being 'serious'.

The modern theatre has traditionally become associated only with entertainment. What goes on there is most usually and most indicatively described as a 'show'. Many serious and intelligent people consider that a theatrical performance can only be frivolous and is almost certain to be licentious as well. Moreover, our performance was being offered for sale commercially. The artistic intention certainly was serious and certainly was religious. But the fact remains that the priests and acolytes were being quite well paid for their services, and the members of the congregation were expected to cough up a substantial price for the privilege of attendance. In these circumstances the comfort and convenience of the audience had to have a higher consideration than if the occasion had been in every sense a religious festival, and the routine of the performance simply had to conform in certain respects to current commercial practice.

One of these respects which was felt to matter a great deal was the length of the performance. It is generally expected that the public will be entertained for a space of time that varies between two and three hours. It may seem very silly that this should be important. But if a play lasts for more than three hours, people get tired and fussed about late transport or being late to bed. If it lasts less than two hours and a half they feel cheated of their money's worth.

The *Oedipus* of Sophocles, in our production, lasts ninety minutes. We knew very well that if our audience had been offered a performance as brief as this, no matter what the quality, it would have felt extremely dissatisfied. So, in addition to other more serious, more practical

OLD MEN
OF THE
CHORUS

and more respectable reasons, an intermission was required to pad out the performance to a length more in conformity with the current practice of show business.

The practical problem, then, was how to effect this intermission with the least damage to the dignity and continuity of the tragedy.

By the end of Jocasta's prayer, the Queen, her attendant and all the Chorus were on their knees. Unseen by the audience, at the head of one of the aisles of the theatre, the Man from Corinth gave a great and cheerful cry of 'News! Good news!' All on the stage turned, surprised and expectant, towards the source of the cry. And then, as they rose from their knees, the stage-lights dimmed. Under cover of a moment of darkness, the actors left the stage. When the house-lights came on, it was empty.

Then, at the end of the intermission, the house-lights went out and in the darkness the actors again took up their stations, not, however, at the same place they had reached before the intermission. When the stage-lights came on they were in position to speak the chorus which follows the confession of Oedipus. Jocasta made her entrance again. The prayer was made again. But this time, after the cry of 'News', the Man from Corinth came down the aisle, was welcomed by the Chorus, led to the Queen, and the play proceeded.

By this means the second part of the play got off to a flying start. Actors and audience were given the moment of recapitulation to re-establish contact, re-establish something of the impetus which the first part of the play had generated.

The device did not entirely heal the gaping wound made by the intermission in the play's continuity; but it did at least suggest that a feeling of continuity was being sought. In practical terms it meant that the audience had time to 'settle' before the Man from Corinth

OEDIPUS

JOCASTA

THE OLD SHEPHERD

THE MAN FROM CORINTH

began his scene, before there was new material to assimilate.

The Corinthian had a round, jolly, smiling, simpleton's face; in size and texture his mask resembled those of the Chorus. To show that he had made a journey, that he was an outsider, he carried a powerful staff and had a big hat slung on his back. He was played as a hearty, countrified fellow, quite unaware, until too late, of the deadly nature of his news.

THE SECOND PART

WHEN OEDIPUS RETURNED, he crept on to the stage furtively, fearfully, in strong contrast to the royal and confident manner of earlier entrances. For a moment the news of the death of Polybus seems to promise relief, then suddenly fear is only further confirmed and it begins to look likely that he has not only murdered his father but that the other and even more horrible prediction of the oracle is about to be fulfilled, that he is living as his mother's husband.

To Jocasta the frightful truth is inescapable. The anguish of her realization is one of the great moments of the play, of all drama. The refusal by Oedipus to recognize the depth of this anguish, his pretense that it is merely an outburst of petulant dynastic pride by Jocasta is extremely hard to accept. It is only possible to make it plausible if it is part of the wild exaltation which now takes hold of the King, and which expresses powerfully the way human consciousness refuses to face a reality which is too unpleasant to be borne, until the confrontation is entirely inevitable.

This passage, in which Oedipus, flying from reality, takes refuge in the fantastic notion that he is the child of Good Luck, is one of the greatest of many great strokes

162

of insight in the play. Just so, we are led to believe, did Hitler behave in the last phase. Reality is too terrible to contemplate; fear must be compensated by the fantasy of an imaginary identity more splendid than the real one, and an easy and agreeable future arranged by Destiny —a mother figure.

In a kind of delirium, utterly unable to face the idea of his real mother's identity, Oedipus invokes a fictitious and supernatural mother. In the same breath that he upbraids Jocasta for dynastic pride, he is claiming kinship with the years, with the months. The years, be it noted, are periods of time measured by the number of revolutions the sun makes round the earth; the moon shines only in the light of the sun god. All this new-claimed kindred of Oedipus have in common their dependence upon the sun. All unawares Oedipus is asserting his kinship with that very sun god who is about to destroy him.

At the same time, the Chorus of Thebans catch the exaltation of their King. They too turn to a mother figure but not, like Oedipus, to Good Luck or to Deity. The Thebans turn to Cithaeron, the mountain which dominates their city. It is often the case that a landmark, natural or man-made, acquires great symbolic importance and a personality like that of an older friend or a substitute parent. To thousands of Londoners during the air-raids of 1940-45, St. Paul's Cathedral became a symbol, a personalization of Mother London, and the voice of Big Ben proclaiming the hours so regularly, in a tone so constant, so reliable, so familiar, was the voice of a dear and greatly respected elder brother.

So now in this strange and irrational moment of excitement, the Thebans invoke Mount Cithaeron. Oedipus, whom hitherto they had regarded as a great man, almost a god, but a foreigner, is now revealed as one

163

of Theban origin, one of themselves. Infected by his ecstasy, they hail the mother-mountain; they praise Oedipus as the son of one of the mountain-nymphs begotten in a hidden glen (a striking reiteration of the glen image) of Cithaeron by Pan, Apollo, or Dionysus.

The feeling of this chorus is ecstatic. It is a raising of Oedipus to the heights, before he is dashed into the abyss. It is a moment analogous to the time in a sacrifice when the victim is crowned with garlands just before the knife is placed across its throat. It is the ride to Jerusalem on Palm Sunday.

We endeavoured to make this chorus extremely primitive. There was chanting, stamping, much fawning and flopping before Oedipus. The chorus itself was very softly spoken, moving imperceptibly from speech to the sustained melodic line of a two-part chorale which faded again back into speech and thence to silence. Oedipus stood with raised arms and uplifted head in the centre of a cluster of prostrate adorers. The group was held for a moment motionless and silent. Then Oedipus, turning his head, lowering his arms, seemed to feel the approach of the Old Shepherd.

The Old Shepherd was a tiny bowed figure. His face was round and wrinkled and dark, sunburned to a deep mahogany. The head was covered with little white woolly curls, and over his shoulders was a white woolly cape. He was led by two guards very, very slowly down a long aisle to the stage. When he approached the stage the old men of the Chorus surrounded him in silence and he was lifted very gently and slowly and deposited in front of the King. The movement was not in the least realistic, but it did, we think, powerfully and movingly, present this confrontation of Oedipus with his Destiny, in the form of this tiny, bowed and trembling figure.

The brief and terrible scene of question and answer between King and Shepherd was played very quietly, with no theatrical fireworks, no climax.

Finally, face to face with irrefutable proof of his identity and his guilt, the King paused a short while. There was a hush in every audience who saw the play that was like the deathly stillness before thunder. Then with a low moan he acknowledged his own accursedness, took farewell of the light, and withdrew into the shadows of the palace. In fading light the Chorus mourned for him.

THE MESSENGER

In an endeavour to make this an entirely ritualistic expression and to remove it from the particularity of private grief, it was spoken in unison, rather as the prayers are chanted in a High Anglican liturgy, by tenors and basses antiphonally. The grouping was no less formal. This did, we think, give it an effect primarily musical and only secondarily emotional. The audience had been asked to share a long spell of emotional tension. This chorus must provide a rest without breaking the mood, must voice the audience's pity, but must do so formally, gravely, without tears or passion. It must be a quiet bridge from the catastrophe to the Messenger's narration of violence and horror. By the end of the chorus the stage was nearly dark. The figures were no more than mourning, chanting shadows.

The Messenger was heard, rather than seen, to emerge from the palace, clinging to the walls, clutching at the pillars, an entirely black figure with a contorted mask of grief and horror coloured like pewter or lead. His narration describes the suicide of Jocasta, the discovery of her body by Oedipus, and how he blinds himself. As in the scene between Jocasta and Oedipus which we have considered at length, the details of this speech are all symbolic, all have a second meaning. We do not propose to discuss them. They confirmed us in our opinion that the play must be symbolically and not literally interpreted; but nothing that is said here affected the visual scheme.

THE USE OF LIGHTING

It has been a matter of some concern to us how far to use light on the Stratford stage as a decoration and a means of enhancing atmosphere, as opposed to a merely utilitarian source of illumination.

It has always been our view that one should not be doctrinaire or dogmatic, partly because dogmatism is never a good idea, and partly because doctrines can, on this topic, reach opposing conclusions. It is possible to maintain that an apron-stage and an auditorium in arena form are denials of the idea of theatrical illusion and that, therefore, lighting must not be used for illusionary purposes. But it seems to us that 'fancy' lighting need not necessarily have an illusionary purpose. It can be used, for instance, to place emphasis here or there on the stage, or for purely decorative purposes, or as an aid to atmosphere, even if only by the cliché method of bright light for cheerful scenes, dim light for scenes which are melancholy or mysterious. To use dim light to suggest evening, however, seems to us the wrong, the illusionary idea. Partly through being in doubt about this, partly, let us admit, because the lighting plant at Stratford is rather inexpensive and therefore rather inflexible, we

166

have hitherto confined ourselves to nothing more elaborate than an occasional unobtrusive dimming or checking of light on certain occasions when it seemed appropriate—the romantic finales, for instance, in Shakespearean comedy, the battle scenes in *Richard III* and *Julius Caesar*, the prison scenes in *Measure for Measure*.

The final scenes of *Oedipus* were played in a considerable degree of dimness for several purposes: first, for the rather obvious reason of enhancing a romantic, and therefore probably inappropriate and over-sentimental atmosphere of melancholy; second, and more defensibly, as a symbol of the spiritual darkness descending upon Thebes and the physical blindness descending upon the King; third, to mark visually as well as musically the fact that the catastrophe of the play is succeeded by a long declining movement, a quiet *decrescendo*. Finally, there was the practical consideration that the visual detail of Oedipus' blinding must not be realistic but that we had not quite sufficient confidence in our stylistic solution of this problem to expose it to harsh light and detailed scrutiny.

We had both seen this blindness realistically suggested. Laurence Olivier had played the part with deserved and immense acclaim. But when he re-entered for this final scene festooned with plastic streams of crimson lake, which elaborately attempted, but utterly failed, to suggest rivers of blood pouring from ruined sockets, we had both felt that the attempt was mistaken not only in practice but in theory. It was exposing what had been deliberately concealed by the author from the sight of the audience; it was doing again what had been done better in the words of the Messenger. By forcing the audience's attention, but not its conviction, upon the material details of the blinding, it was detracting attention from the spiritual meaning. An incomplete and unsuccessful realistic effect was replacing the immeasurably greater imaginative possibility of a symbol.

How was this symbolic effect to be achieved?

We cannot tell whether or no our attempt was satisfactory. It certainly had one merit: extreme simplicity. The King wore an immense and shapeless robe of dark purplish crimson, in thick woollen material. The head and face were covered with a thick veil of black fishing-net. By this means there would be, we hoped, an indirect association, through colour, with blood; the ruined face and head were concealed but in such a way that the actor could see, that his speech would not be muffled; and, not least important with a long and exacting scene to play, he could take deep and unimpeded breaths.

THE LAST SCENE

THE FINAL SCENE, with its long and apparently, self-pitying expressions of grief, its long recapitulation of Oedipus' misdeeds like one of the public confessions in Dostoevski, its long insistence upon funerary formalities, its long dwelling upon the unfortunate position of the daughters—all this is very far removed from the sort of attitude to disaster which we now expect a hero to show. There is none of the decent reticence, the stiff upper lip which in contemporary Western society is expected of a soldier and a gentleman. There is no Christian resignation and little Christian fortitude. There is nothing of that much-admired attitude of a bloodhound by Landseer—faithful red-rimmed doggy eyes turned trustingly upwards towards a kind master. But then Apollo has not been shown as a kind master, a benign father, a wise counsellor or reliable friend. It is questionable if the Deity has been shown in even so sympathetic a light as a remote and disinterested force. The

OEDIPUS BLIND

trusting upward gaze could only seem in the context either hypocritical or idiotic.

Perhaps the hardest thing of all to apprehend is the long-drawn lament over the children. In realistic terms one is irritated by its selfishness and tactlessness. Daddy is making things so much worse for the poor dears. And, anyway, haven't we all known children to survive a disastrous start in life? They are young enough to begin a new life in a totally different environment with a placid, kind adopted Auntie who will have enough sense to ask no awkward questions. But all such ideas are trivial and irrelevant and provincial. They assume that Greek manners are, or ought to be, the same as our own. They fail to assume the preconceptions of the audience for whom the play was written. This family, to the Athenian audience, was clearly and irrevocably doomed and polluted. There was absolutely no possibility for a new and happier life for Ismene and Antigone. Their fate was part of the symbolic curse hanging over their symbolically polluted house.

But surely one may legitimately wonder why there should be such an amount of horror over a parricide which, in rational terms, was obviously accidental. Certainly Oedipus was morally to blame for killing Laius, and even more so for killing his servants. But in terms of modern justice there would be more than a chance of a verdict not of murder but of manslaughter. The crime was not premeditated and there was evidence of considerable provocation. Equally, the horror over the incest seems to be excessive, if regarded rationally.

This is not the place for a general discussion on the propriety of our contemporary moral and judicial attitude to incest. It would appear to be a crime which is regarded in contemporary society with a remarkably primitive degree of horror and blame, surrounded by secrecy and superstition, removed by tacit and almost universal agreement from the realm of rational consideration. But since the incest of Oedipus and Jocasta was committed entirely unwittingly there can, in their case, be no question of blame or guilt or shame. The horror is not a particular one arraigning these two guilty individuals. It is an expression of horror at the idea of incest in general. It is presented in this play as one of the ultimates in Pollution.

THE FREUDIAN INTERPRETATION

Now, CLEARLY, if the play is rightly to be regarded, as we regard it, as an allegory, a series of symbolic events occurring to symbolic persons in symbolic environments, then any intelligent person must wonder how to interpret not only such subsidiary symbols as Laius' carriage, the meeting of three ways, Jocasta's self-slaughter by hanging, or Oedipus dashing in the doors of her marriage-chamber which was also her death-chamber. It is even more important, and far harder, to find the meaning of the three or four great symbolic themes round which the tragedy is constructed—pollution, parricide, incest, blindness, or darkness, contrasted with light. Perhaps the most important and the most baffling symbol of all is Apollo.

Here, of course, is the place where it would be great to come out with a notable discovery, to utter the last irrefutable word, to confound previous critics and amaze those yet unborn, to interpret satisfyingly, completely, once and for all, this majestic and fascinating enigma.

But even for the interpretation of riddles Sophocles offers a rather ominous symbol. The Sphinx propounded a riddle. Oedipus supplied the answer. It is true that this delivered Thebes from the Sphinx, who dived off a rock and never was seen again. But for Thebes, Sphinx was succeeded by pestilence. And just look what happened to Oedipus!

In our epoch it is quite hard to look for our solution in other than Freudian terms. Freud has revolutionized our conception of ourselves, and one of the pillars of the Freudian edifice is the Oedipus complex. It is all too easy to think because of its topicality that this is what the tragedy is about; and certainly it is one of the themes. But surely the relation of Oedipus to Jocasta and Laius is far less important than his relation to Apollo. The tragedy is about Man and God and only secondarily about Child and Parent. In other words, psychology must not, in our view, be allowed to overshadow theology.

It is noticeable that the father-son relation, though important to the play, is never applied to the connection of Apollo with mortals. Apollo is never presented as a father figure, nor is any mention made of a father god, a conception which was as familiar to the Greeks as to the Jews, or to ourselves, or to any patriarchal society.

It is true that under stress of great emotion, as we have seen, Oedipus does appeal to a fictitious mother goddess, Good Luck or Chance. Incidentally, is it intended that at this moment he appeals to a deity who is traditionally represented as blind? There is, however, no suggestion whatever that this particular speech represents any serious theological idea, on the part of either Oedipus or Sophocles.

Therefore, while our opinion is anything but definite, and can only be advanced with great diffidence, we think that theologically the symbolism of the play does not relate God to Man as a parent; it suggests the Immanence of God in Man, or perhaps, more widely and vaguely, the Immanence of God in Nature.

There is, we suggest, a strong and repeated suggestion of scepticism about priesthood and oracles. Tiresias, although right in what he says about Oedipus, is not a sympathetic portrait; the scene greatly misses irony unless he is presented as a disreputable kind of fakir. Again the pronouncement which Creon brings from Delphi at the beginning of the play, and the Delphic prophecies first to Laius and then to Oedipus, which had been made before the events of the play, all turn out to be true, but so confusedly and unhelpfully uttered that, in point of fact, instead of preventing they precipitate the havoc. Delphi, in short, like Tiresias, is presented unsympathetically.

It used to be almost a commonplace, when the religious implications of this play were discussed, to say that Apollo was punishing Oedipus for ὕβρις, for uppishness, for not knowing his place in the universe. This argument would be more impressive if there were more evidence of the uppishness of Oedipus. But, on the evidence of this play, he behaves with exemplary piety and humility towards Apollo, exemplary justice and humanity as a monarch. His conduct as a husband and father cannot be faulted. It is true that he is rude to Tiresias, and to Creon he is both unreasonable and unkind. But these offences are both rather lapses of manners than of morals and are committed, the first under stress of great provocation by Tiresias, the second under the stress of great perturbation. The sum of the two offences seems entirely insufficient to weigh in the scale of justice against the frightful punishments which they are supposed to have earned. Moreover, this simple moral explanation of the story derives from its facts, and not at all from the symbols with which we have been concerned.

The symbolism seems to suggest that the play certainly is concerned with Man's search for his own identity, largely in terms of 'Who is my father? Who is my mother?' But it is also no less concerned with the question 'Who is responsible? Who is answerable?'

Implicitly, by disparaging Tiresias and Delphi, Sophocles rejects a simple childlike dependence upon a God outside ourselves. Yet, when the Leader of the Chorus directly asks Oedipus who is responsible for the terrible act of self-blinding, the answer, without apparent bitterness, without passion, is categorical: 'It is Apollo.' And at an earlier point in the play Oedipus cries, 'O God, what have you planned to do to me?' Oedipus, we must suppose, did believe that there was a power outside himself which was executing a prearranged plan.

But are we on this account to believe that Sophocles felt the same? It is a common mistake of criticism to think that a dramatic author necessarily puts his own beliefs into the mouths of his creatures. His own beliefs are implicit rather than explicit in his work.

In this play, we believe, Sophocles expresses his own beliefs not at all on the factual, literal plane, but through a language of symbols. While Oedipus is Everyman, nevertheless obviously Everyman does not murder his father and live as his mother's husband. The parricide and the incest are, as every student of Freud believes, symbols of attachment of sons to their mothers, with a consequent jealousy and hostility to their fathers. That this attachment and this hostility of Oedipus were connected with persons whom he did not know to be his father and mother, symbolizes the fact that these emotions are not conscious.

But the parricide and the incest are only two, and not necessarily the two most important, as they are certainly not the two most emphatically or frequently stated symbols in this play. We consider that the symbols of light-darkness dominate the play. And we consider that this must be interpreted as sight-blindness and thence insight-ignorance. We also consider that the connection between Apollo and Light is inescapable and that it is highly significant that this particular deity dominates the play, is related explicitly to every twist and turn of the plot, and is explicitly acknowledged by Oedipus as the planner and executor of his fate.

We do not feel able to do more than draw attention to the dominance of the light-darkness motif, and to hazard the speculation—no more—that interpretation may be sought in connection with the doctrine of immanent deity, the light within ourselves.

More and more as we worked on the play, as in rehearsal we lived in it, absorbing it not so much rationally or even emotionally, but as a pianist absorbs music which has to be practised over and over and over, we became convinced that the conflict in the play was between Oedipus and Immanent Apollo, God within himself.

The tragedy would in that case, like Hamlet, be a tragedy of self-conflict. Oedipus, like Hamlet, is from beginning to end the focus of attention, is carefully, elaborately and sympathetically presented as a 'character'. But he does not consciously guide the events of the tragedy. A situation is postulated, in both *Hamlet* and *Oedipus*; it concerns a murdered father. But in both cases, though the central character acts with extraordinary intelligence, consistency and vigour (the notion that Hamlet cannot take action simply is not supported by the evidence of the play), nevertheless his decisions are all forced upon him against his conscious inclination. He is swept to destruction upon a tide of predestination.

In *Oedipus* the problem, we suggest, is how to relate the plot-motifs of parricide and incest to the philosophy which finds expression in the complex of ideas symbolized by Apollo.

God within ourselves implies that each individual has some responsibility for his own actions. Parents—the 'second parties' in the motif of parricide-incest—are also

175

connected with the idea of responsibility. At some period the responsible man must take over the control of his own life from his father, must, in symbolical terms, smite Laius from his chariot; and at some period he must be confronted with the incestuous implications of his relation to his mother.

Can it be that the main theme of the play is the emergence of man from darkness to light by the assumption of responsibilities which in darker or more primitive stages of development are delegated to 'outside' authorities—parents and non-immanent gods?

A LITERAL INTERPRETATION NOT ENOUGH

NOW BACK TO PRACTICAL MATTERS of production: Working at the last scenes of the play with two differently gifted but serious and intelligent actors, we have come to the confident conclusion that a mere literal following of the lines is not the clue to the interpretation.

It is apparent that the first speeches with the Chorus after the blinding have some further implication than self-pity and mourning. There is, we all felt, a sense of exaltation as well as of suffering. Perhaps there is something analogous to the glory of expiation upon which Roman Catholic hagiology insists. Certainly, the actor here must try to catch the note not of self-pity but of rapt exaltation.

Then comes the invocation recalling Cithaeron, Corinth, the three roads, the secret glen, the narrow way and, later in the same speech, the marriage bed. It will, we think, have been apparent that the drift of the speech was ritualistic, was a ceremonial recapitulation of crucial events in his life, a ceremonial invocation of the localities with which these events were connected. The conjunction of these words with gestures of washing may perhaps have suggested to a few spectators that this, like Lady Macbeth's handwashing, like the ritual bath in Caesar's blood, like Christian baptism, was a ceremony of purification. The idea of purification by blood is not exclusively pagan. The well-known hymn by William Cowper strikingly relates it to Christian practice:

> There is a fountain filled with blood,
> Drawn from Emmanuel's veins,
> And sinners plunged beneath that flood
> Lose all their guilty stains.

When Creon entered he was accompanied by armed guards, wore the crown and carried the sceptre formerly used by Oedipus, and suggested by his demeanour that he was in the presence of an unclean and polluted thing.

The children wore sad, flat little masks and long shapeless robes in two shades of crimson. When they joined Oedipus the three figures merged into one single three-shaded crimson mass, and his speech to them deploring their fate was accompanied by a slow, tangling, weaving dance. This was again to insist upon the ritual, rather than realistic, nature of the speech, and to suggest the oneness of the three. The girls moved as if tied to their father; they were three trunks growing out of one twisted, tortured root.

At the end the children were torn from him by guards —a slow, heavy movement, one child dragged, the other lifted into the air, slowly, slowly, and in silence. Then Creon withdrew.

Oedipus was alone on the stage, the Chorus hidden in the shadows. Very slowly Oedipus withdrew from the lighted area, down the steps, down a slope, always downward, out of sight. As he moved from the sight of the audience the Chorus slowly mounted the steps into the dim light of the stage and, standing motionless, monumental, spoke very simply and quietly and unemotionally the five terse powerful lines which are Yeats' version of the final chorus.

This essay will close as it began with a word of apology that our scholarship is not more adequate to the task of interpreting this masterpiece, and of hope that to some few readers it may be of interest to possess a record of the way a production is prepared. When a building is erected there must first be a scaffolding to support the workmen. So in the production of a play those who put it together in rehearsal must be supported on a previously erected scaffolding of theory and meditation translated into practical plans.

It is such a scaffolding that we have here endeavoured to describe.

Thrice the Brinded Cat Hath Mew'd

WAS SET IN LINOTYPE BASKERVILLE 11 ON 13

AND THE TEXT PRINTED FROM TYPE

BY MCCORQUODALE & BLADES (CANADA) LIMITED, TORONTO.

COLOUR SEPARATIONS FROM MISS MOISEIWITSCH'S SKETCHES

BY GARBE-COLLINS LIMITED, TORONTO,

LITHOGRAPHED BY ASHTON-POTTER LIMITED, TORONTO.

BOUND BY J. W. DEYELL PRINTERS LTD., LINDSAY.

TITLE PAGE BY NANCY CAUDLE